THE MODERN
LANGUAGE
OF ARCHITECTURE

By Bruno Zevi

University of Washington Press
Seattle and London

Part I, "A Guide to the Anticlassical Code," was translated by Ronald Strom
from pages 1–84 of *Il linguaggio moderno dell'architettura,* Piccola Biblioteca Einaudi
214, copyright © 1973 Giulio Einaudi editore s.p.a., Turin, Part II, "Architecture
versus Architectural History," was translated by William A. Packer from
Architettura e storiografia, Piccola Biblioteca Einaudi 216, copyright © 1974 Giulio
Einaudi editore s.p.a., Turin. The two parts formed the basis of two Walker-
Ames Lectures delivered at the University of Washington, Seattle, on January
27 and February 1, 1977.

Library of Congress Cataloging in Publication Data
Zevi, Bruno, 1918-
    The modern language of architecture.
    Translated from the author's Il linguaggio moderno dell'architettura, and Archi-
tettura e storiografia.
    "The two parts formed the basis of two Walker-Ames lectures delivered at
the University of Washington, Seattle, on January 27 and February 1, 1977."
    Includes index.
    1. Architecture—Terminology. 2. Architecture—Historiography. I. Zevi,
Bruno, 1918- Il linguaggio moderno dell'architettura. II. Zevi, Bruno, 1918-
Architettura e storiografia. III. Title.
NA31.Z48   720'.1'4   77-3829
ISBN 0-295-95568-6

Contents

Illustrations

PART ONE: *A Guide to the Anticlassical Code*

Introduction: *Speaking Architecture*

In 1964 John Summerson published a short book entitled *The Classical Language of Architecture,* which has been very successful throughout the world. I waited a decade for its logical and necessary sequel, "The Anticlassical Language of Architecture" or, rather, "The Modern Language of Architecture," but neither Summerson nor anyone else wrote it. Why not? One can imagine a host of daunting reasons. Nevertheless the gap needs filling. It is the most urgent task facing architectural history and criticism today. It cannot be postponed, it is already long overdue.

Without a language, we cannot speak. What is more, it is language that "speaks us," in the sense that it provides the instruments of communication without which it would be impossible even to work out our thoughts. Yet in the course of centuries only one architectural language has been codified, that of classicism. None other has been processed and put into the systematic form required of an acknowledged language. All were considered exceptions to the rule, the classical rule, and not alternatives to it, with a life of their own. Even modern architecture, which emerged in reaction against neoclassicism, runs the risk of reverting to stale Beaux-Arts archetypes unless it is structured into a language.

This is an incredible and absurd situation. We are squandering a colossal heritage of expression because we shirk the responsibility of transcribing it and making it transmissible. It may not be very long before we forget how to *speak architecture* at all. Indeed, most people who are designing and building today can barely mumble. They utter inarticulate meaningless sounds that carry no message. They do not know how to speak. They say nothing and have nothing to say. There is an even more serious danger facing us. If the modern movement is ever jettisoned, we may

3

no longer be able to read the images of any architects who have spoken a language other than classicism: the images of the Stone Age, late antiquity and the Middle Ages, the works of the Mannerists, Michelangelo, Borromini, the Arts and Crafts movement and Art Nouveau, Wright, Loos, Le Corbusier, Gropius, Mies, Aalto, Scharoun, and the younger men from Johansen to Safdie.

Nobody uses the classical orders today. But classicism is a state of mind that goes beyond the "orders" and stultifies even those discourses which are uttered using anticlassical nouns and verbs. The Beaux-Arts system actually codified Gothic, then Romanesque, Baroque, Egyptian, Japanese, and finally modern architecture by a very simple expedient: it put them on ice by classicizing their free structure. Surely, if it should prove impossible to formulate the modern idiom in truly dynamic fashion, it would go the same suicidal way, which is what more than one wretched critic and/or architect wishes would happen.

It is therefore essential that we try to codify the modern language at once, without looking for a priori solutions to all the theoretical problems involved. Abstract theories are often an alibi for further delays. Dozens of books and hundreds of essays have discussed the question of whether or not architecture can be treated as a language, whether nonverbal languages have a double articulation (or dual patterning), and whether the attempt at codifying modern architecture might not block its development. Semiology is certainly essential, but by itself it cannot solve architectural problems. For better or worse, architects communicate. And the fact remains that they speak architecture, whether it is a language or not. Thus we must set down precisely what it implies to speak architecture in an anticlassical key. If we can do this, the theoretical apparatus will come by itself as we proceed with our work.

There are thousands of architects and students of architecture designing without knowing the vocabulary, the grammar, and the syntax of the contemporary language, which are, in fact, a kind of antivocabulary, antigrammar, and antisyntax in relation to classicism. Critical judgments are being made on two levels, in the profession and in the schools. But what standards are used? And are they legitimate? This is the challenge that faces us, both as producers and as consumers of architecture. If we are going to understand one another, we must use the same terms and agree on their meaning. The problem seems enormous only because it has been so little investigated until now.

Ours is an intentionally provocative goal: to establish a series of "invariables" in the modern language of architecture, based on the most significant and challenging buildings. A question might arise. Some code is indispensable in verbal communication; otherwise there is a danger of not communicating at all. In architecture, however, anyone can dispense with it at will, without having to give up building for this reason. Of course, he can design even in Babylonian style if he wants to, but all he can communicate are his own neuroses.

I have discussed the question of architectural language with scholars, practicing architects, and most often with anxious and confused students, quite bewildered by the fact that nobody teaches them an idiom they can speak. A single conclusion came out of these conversations: although there are excellent excuses for not facing such a difficult and painful problem, the present impasse must be overcome and a beginning made.

This book is even shorter than Summerson's. Only seven invariables are analyzed. One could add ten more, or twenty, or fifty, so long as they do not contradict the first seven. The validity of this approach must be tested on the drawing board and on real buildings. Everyone can set about checking this "basic language." And it should come as no surprise that, out of a hundred buildings erected nowadays, ninety prove to be altogether anachronistic works that belong somewhere between the Renaissance and Beaux-Arts, while eight have some incoherent elements of modern "style," and, in the best of circumstances, maybe two are merely ungrammatical, that is to say, they do not speak the old language, but neither do they speak the new one. And that is not all. Even the great masters of the modern movement have sometimes produced regressive classicist works. Thus one cannot help asking, what kind of language is this, if no one or very few people can speak it? Let me answer with another question: how could the modern language of architecture be widely spoken without a code?

These pages have the same goal as any other heretical act: to arouse dissent. If they provoke argument, they will have achieved their aim. Instead of talking endlessly *about* architecture, we shall finally begin to speak architecture.*

1. The dictatorship of the straight line (cartoon by Mauris). It is responsible for the mania of parallels, proportions, chessboard layouts, and right angles— the lexicon, grammar, and syntax of classicism. The monuments of so-called "classical" antiquity have been manhandled to conform to this abstract a priori ideology.

* Four years after the publication of the Italian edition of this book, a most amusing essay by Charles Jencks has been published with the title *The Language of Post-Modern Architecture* (New York: Rizzoli, 1977). It shows that the post-modern, opposing the modern, goes back to the pre-modern, that is, to academic classicism. Perhaps this book should be retitled, "The Post-Post-Modern Language of Architecture."

I

Listing as Design Methodology

The list, or inventory, of functions is the generating principle of the modern language in architecture, and it subsumes all other principles. Listing marks the ethical and operational dividing line between those who speak in modern terms and those who chew on dead languages. Every error, every involution, every psychological lapse and mental block at the drawing table can be traced back, without exception, to a failure to respect this principle. Therefore it is the basic invariable of the contemporary code.

Implicit in listing, or compiling an inventory of functions, is the dismantling and critical rejection of classical rules, "orders," a priori assumptions, set phrases, and conventions of every type and kind. The inventory springs from an act of cultural annihilation—what Roland Barthes calls "the zero degree of writing"—and leads to a rejection of all traditional norms and canons. It demands a new beginning, as if no linguistic system had ever existed before, as if it were the first time in history that we had to build a house or a city.

The list is an ethical principle even before it becomes an operational one. Indeed, with tremendous effort and immense joy, we must strip away the cultural taboos we have inherited. We must track them down one by one in our minds and desanctify them. For the modern architect, the paralyzing taboos are dogmas, conventions, inertia, all the dead weight accumulated during centuries of classicism. By destroying every institutionalized model, he can break free from idolatry. He can reconstruct and relive the whole process of man's formation and development, realizing that more than once in the course of the millennia, architects have wiped the slate clean and erased every grammatical and syntactical rule. In fact, genuinely creative spirits have always started from scratch. The modern revolution is not unprecedented or apocalyptic. There has been a recurrent struggle against repressive bonds throughout the ages.

Listing, going back to the zero degree, makes you rethink architectural semantics. In the beginning, verbs and conjunctions must be eliminated. Words can no longer be used unless their content and meaning have been analyzed in depth. Some examples will get us to the heart of this methodology of design.

Windows. In the classical tradition a module is selected for the openings of a Renaissance or pseudo-Renaissance building. Then the sequence of modules is examined, along with the relationship between full and empty surface areas. Finally, the horizontal and vertical alignments, that is, the superimposition of the orders, are established. Fortunately the modern architect is free of these formalistic concerns. He is engaged in a more complex and rewarding task of resemanticization. First of all, no repetitive modules. Every window is a word that stands for itself, what it means and what it does. It is not something to be aligned or proportioned. It may be any shape—rectangular, square, round, elliptical, triangular, composite, or free profile. Depending on the room it must light, the window may be anything from a long narrow strip at ceiling or floor level to a cut in the wall or a running band at eye level: whatever may be desired or considered suitable after calculating the specific window's function room by room. There is no reason why every window in a building should be just like the next one and not have a character of its own. Once you get rid of the tyranny of classicism, windows will be all the more effective if they are different and can convey a host of messages.

Classicism breaks the façade into vertical and horizontal sections. But eliminating the juxtaposition and superimposition of modules will make the façade whole again. What is far more important, the façade will become *unfinished.* When the openings— high or low, straight or crooked—are no longer regulated by axial relationships, the façade will cease to be closed and aloof, an end in itself, and begin talking to its surroundings. It will stop

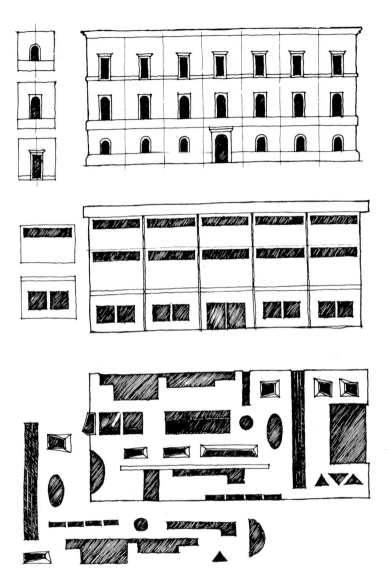

2. The methodology of listing functions, applied to windows. Classicism, whether
old classicism *(above)* or the pseudomodern *(center)*, is concerned with the module,
its repetition, the relationship between full and empty spaces, and alignment. It
is concerned with everything except windows. Listing gives back to every element
its specific meaning *(below)* and then assembles the various elements.

being extraneous and hostile and start taking an active part in the city—or landscape.

Windows are not an appropriate example in discussing modern architecture because, as we will see later, the principle of functional listing precludes the very idea of "façade." Nevertheless, when an architect works in urban fabrics conceived according to preordained schemes and volumes, he is forced to design façades. But that is no reason to give up the modern language. The minute he differentiates windows by form and position, he has done away with the traditional façade and its classical connotations. Indeed, he can inject new life into it by making some windows protrude and others recede, by playing with the thickness of the wall to create a frame of shadow around the glass or, on the contrary, to bring the glass forward into the blaze of light. And why not slant the windows to the surface of the façade? One window can tilt down, focusing on a square, a tree, or a doorway across the street. Another can turn up, framing a piece of sky. A window can be slanted left or right to catch panoramic views, a section of street, a monument, or the sea. Windows can be conceived with a wealth of angles, so that their surfaces are never parallel to the building front.

Even when limited to the detail of windows, the principle of functional listing challenges the classical approach to the façade, takes away its "finished" look, and breaks its square frame by fragmenting the corners of the building and maybe the line between top floor and roof. A double aim is achieved: alternate lighting solutions in the interiors and heightened expressive qualities on the outside.

I can imagine two objections, one of simple dismay and the other of ideological alibis masking dismay. The first objection is that a frightening amount of work is involved in this procedure: if the outline and position of every window have to be thought out separately, the design of a ten-window façade is going to take too much time and energy, far out of proportion to the rewards. The second objection is that such a method may lead to an "academy of misrule," to the triumph of arbitrariness.

The answer to the first objection is that it is largely true. The only correct way to design a window is to study the space it lights, for the perceptual and behavioral value of any space depends on how it is lighted. The fact is that spaces and volumes, the whole building, have to be planned before it is decided what shapes of window to choose. Is modern architecture hard? Probably, but it is splendid because every element, every word of it, is related to a social content. If it were easy, most of the buildings put up today would be truly modern. Suffice it to look at their windows to realize that they are quite often the product of academic irresponsibility.

As to the second objection, that the modern language of architecture tends to be arbitrary: on the contrary, classicism is totally arbitrary, in so far as it gives mythical value to abstract orders that repress freedom and social behavior. Does functional listing lead to disorder? Yes, to sacrosanct disorder that drives out idolatrous order and the taboos imposed by standardized and alienating mass production. The listing method rejects the products of neocapitalist industry, just as William Morris rejected paleocapitalist products in the second half of the nineteenth century. Industry too often promotes sameness; it categorizes, standardizes, and classicizes. Recent skyscrapers with their curtain walls are more static, boxy, and monolithic than those built fifty years ago. You can see it from the windows as well.

The two objections betray troubled psychological origins. The modern language increases the possibilities of choice, while classical architecture reduces them. Choice creates anguish, a neurotic "anxiety for certainty." What is to be done? There are no tranquilizers for this ailment. But are there in other areas? Does not abstract painting arouse a similar anguish? What about dodecaphonic and aleatory or accidental music? And conceptual art? Is it not anguishing to look at oneself in the mirror for the first time and recognize oneself in an image outside oneself, or to learn that the earth rotates even though it seems to be standing still? Fear of freedom and horror of irrational impulses are at the bottom of this anguish. Let us suppose for a moment that, in a given building, windows could be alike or different without altering their function in any way. The modern language says, let them be different, let there be more choices. The classical code dictates that they all be alike, they must be orderly—like corpses. But the hypothesis that they may be equally functional is absurd, really arbitrary. This merely confirms an established fact, but one that is very hard to instill in the minds of architects: what seems rational and logical, because it is regulated and ordered, is humanly and socially foolish; it makes sense only in terms of despotic power. What is presumed irrational, on the other hand, is generally the result of thinking things through and courageously granting the imagination its rights. Classicism is fine for cemeteries, not for life. Only death can resolve the "anxiety of certainty."

What has been said about windows should be repeated for every aspect of design on any scale: volumes and spaces, their interrelationships, urban complexes, and regional planning. The invariable is always the functional list. Why should a room be cubical or prismatic, instead of free form and harmonious with its uses? Why should a group of rooms form a simple box? Why must a building be conceived as the wrapping for a lot of small boxes packed inside a larger box? Why should it be closed in on itself, making a sharp distinction between the architectural cavities and the urban or natural landscape? Why must all the rooms in an apartment be the same height? And so on. The invariable of modern language consists in whys and what-fors, in not submitting to a priori laws, in rethinking every conventional statement, and in the systematic development and verification of new hypotheses. A will to be free of idolatrous precepts is the mainspring of modern architecture, beginning with Le Corbusier's famous five principles: the "free" plan, the "free" façade, the pilotis that leave the ground "free" under the building, the roof garden that implies the "free" use of the top of the building, and even the strip window, in so far as it offers further evidence that the façade is "free" of structural elements.

The list approach continually makes a clean start. It verifies and challenges even the five principles, as Le Corbusier himself did in his later years, from Ronchamp on. Indeed, his earlier "purism" imposed heavy design restrictions, because the plan was "free" only within the perimeter of a "pure" geometric figure. Why should we sanctify geometry, or straight lines, or right angles? The functional list says *no* to these prescriptions as well.

It affects content and form, individual ethics and collective life, just as language does.

The following chapters examine other applications of this invariable. There is no modern architecture outside the list process. The rest is fraud, classicist or pseudomodern. It is a crime, when there is a proper language of architecture to speak.

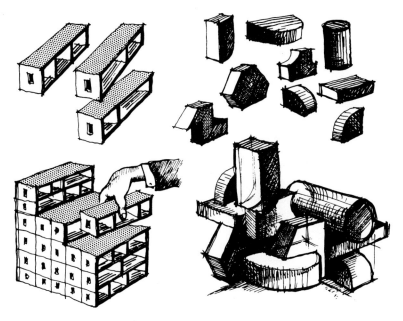

3. The methodology of listing functions, applied to volumes. Old and pseudo-modern classicism boxes man's activities, ignoring their specific differences. Then it sets the boxes above and beside each other to form a larger box *(left)*. Listing gives meaning back to volumes, groups them, but preserving their individuality *(right)*.

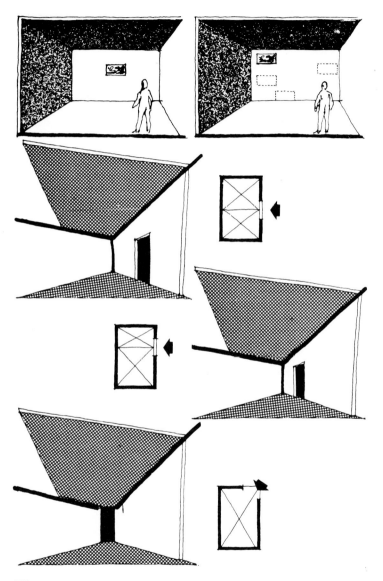

4. Where to hang a picture. Anywhere except in the middle of a wall *(above)*. Where to put a door. Anywhere except in the middle *(center)*. The farther the door is from the middle, the deeper the room will look *(center, below)*. The corner door is the ideal: it enhances the diagonal *(below)*.

II

Asymmetry and Dissonance

Where then? *Anywhere else.* When you criticize something for being symmetrically arranged, and you are asked where else to put it, your answer should be: *anywhere else.* There is only one place that is radically wrong, the place that is selected "spontaneously," dredging up all the atavistic conventions of the subconscious.

We can take an even simpler example than the window to demonstrate this, a picture. Here is a wall. Where shall we hang the picture? In the center, of course. No, *anywhere else.* To the right or left, higher up or lower down, anywhere but there. If you hang the picture in the middle, it splits the wall into two equal parts. It reduces the visual dimensions and makes them trivial. The picture seems to be framed and isolated by the wall, when it could open up the room and give it breathing space.

Symmetry is one of the invariables of classicism. Therefore asymmetry is an invariable of the modern language. Once you get rid of the fetish of symmetry, you will have taken a giant step on the road to a democratic architecture.

Symmetry = economic waste + intellectual cynicism. Any time you see a house consisting of a central core with two symmetrical lateral extensions you can reject it out of hand. What is in the left wing? The living room, perhaps. And in the right one? Bedrooms and bathrooms. Is there any conceivable reason why the two enveloping volumes should be identical? The architect wasted space by enlarging the living room to make it the same size as the bedrooms. Or else he restricted essential functions of the sleeping area to keep it the same size as the living room. And look at the height of the ceilings. Why should a vast living room

5. Rome, Piazza Venezia. The old narrow square *(above)* could have accommodated an evocative monument like Le Corbusier's "Open Hand" *(second row, left)*. Instead it was blasted open to make room for the pharaonic Victor Emmanuel Monument *(right and third row)*. Of course, no asymmetry was allowed *(below)*.

have a low ceiling? On the other hand, if the bedroom ceiling is too high, the space seems visually cramped and suffocating. It is a flagrant waste, both economically and esthetically; a double injury and a double sacrifice. On the altar of what taboo is this sacrifice laid? On the altar of symmetry.

Symmetry = a spasmodic need for security, fear of flexibility, indetermination, relativity, and growth—in short, fear of living. The schizophrenic cannot bear the temporal aspect of living. To keep his anguish under control, he requires immobility. Classicism is the architecture of conformist schizophrenia. Symmetry = passivity or, in Freudian terms, homosexuality. This is explained by psychoanalysts. *Homo*logous parts instead of *hetero*nymous parts. It is infantile fear of the father—the academy, in this case, is a father figure, protective of the cowardly child—who will castrate you if you attack a heteronymous figure, the woman, the mother. As soon as one becomes passive and accepts symmetry, the anguish seems to subside, because the father no longer threatens, he possesses.

Perhaps the whole history of architecture could be reread in terms of symmetry neurosis. Certainly that of Western architecture could be. It is no accident, for example, that Italy was the first country to revive the worship of this idol during the Renaissance, while other countries continued to develop the Gothic style. The economy of the Italian peninsula was going through a severe crisis which the dominant classes tried to conceal behind a classicist mask. They evoked the Greco-Roman past in a mythical key in order to camouflage the instability of the present. They assumed a courtly, forbidding, or Olympian air to hide the desolation of society. It has always been like that: symmetry is the façade of sham power trying to appear invulnerable. The public buildings of Fascism, Nazism, and Stalinist Russia are all symmetrical. Those of South American dictatorships are symmetrical. Those of theocratic institutions are symmetrical; they often have a double symmetry. Can you imagine an asymmetrical Victor Emmanuel Monument in Rome, out of balance, varied in its parts, with an equestrian statue to the left or right rather than in the center? An Italy capable of building that kind of monument would have been another kind of nation, one committed to the creation of a democratic state administration, an efficient service sector, a society balanced between northern and southern regions and based on justice. As a matter of fact, such a country would not have wasted public funds on a marble monstrosity like the Victor Emmanuel Monument. Such a society would not have disfigured the Piazza Venezia with something that made its proportions so trivial, by moving the Palazzetto Venezia and tearing down the Palazzo Torlonia; in short, ruining not only an architectural hub but the whole townscape of Rome. It would have used the money to build lower-class housing, schools, and libraries and to reform agriculture and public health facilities. The Victor Emmanuel Monument reflects the fragility of a backward nation that pretends to be progressive by striking a triumphant, monumental, arrogant, and bombastic attitude. The flame of the Unknown Soldier at the foot of the Arc de Triomphe in Paris and the Cenotaph in London pale in modesty before this horror, whose symmetry rises to titanic heights of wickedness.

There are symmetrical buildings that are not rhetorical, but all rhetorical buildings—symbols of totalitarian power or products of sloth and cynicism—are symmetrical. On closer examination, moreover, nonrhetorical symmetrical buildings prove to be only partially symmetrical, generally only on the main front. This leads to another observation: symmetry has been used in the most obscene way to deform and falsify the arrangement of historic monuments. The most striking example: the Propylaea of the Athenian Acropolis. These have a blasphemously asymmetric plan; but since the Ecole des Beaux-Arts could not admit that such a heretical structure stood at the very entrance to the sanctuary of classicism, Mnesicles' work was displayed as if it were symmetrical. Why? Because in a moment of mental aberration the Greeks had made a mistake, and it had to be corrected. Another example: the Erechtheum, a quite irregular and asymmetrical building, so "modern" that in a way it is a forerunner of Adolf Loos's multileveled Raumplan. What weight did the Erechtheum carry in the Beaux-Arts doctrine? None. It was not symmetrical, so it could serve no purpose.

Take a room, for example. Where should the entrance door be? Anywhere, just so long as it is not in the middle of a wall.

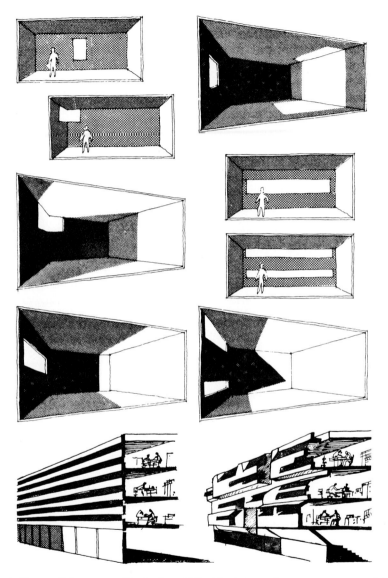

6. How to light a room. Not in the middle *(above)*. Any other arrangement would be better: corner window, strip window, double strip *(center)*. In the Rome railway station, a double glass strip provides light for the offices *(below, left)*, but a greater variety of shapes would have been preferable *(right)*.

That would split the space in two. What "anywhere else" really means is the most conveniently uncentral position, so that the diagonal can be enhanced to create the maximum sense of depth. And to accent the diagonal view, why not detach the entrance door from the wall surface and tilt it? Fine, let us give it a specific meaning, different from the other doors.

The same room. Where should the light come from? Anywhere, as long as it is not in the center of a wall, dividing the room into three sections, an illuminated one between two areas of darkness. Let us give each window new meaning as a specific light carrier in function of the interior space. If there is no view outside, try a strip window at floor level, another one at the ceiling (with a different width to avoid symmetry), and perhaps vertical strips at the corners to light the walls. In the offices of the Rome railway station there are two strips of window per floor, one at desk level and one at the ceiling. This is a satisfactory arrangement, although classicized by too much repetition of the motif. When windows are installed in opposite walls, they must not face each other directly: they will merely light each other and not the room. Take the Room of the Months in the famous Palazzo Schifanoia in Ferrara. Every window faces a full panel on the other side of the room, thus providing magnificent lighting for the marvelous Este frescoes.

Symmetry is a single, though macroscopic, symptom of a tumor whose cells have metastasized everywhere in geometry. The history of cities could be interpreted as the clash between geometry (an invariable of dictatorial or bureaucratic power) and free forms (which are congenial to human life). For hundreds of thousands of years the paleolithic community was ignorant of geometry. But as soon as neolithic settlements began and hunter-cultivators were subjected to a tribal chief, the chessboard made its appearance. Political absolutism imposes geometry, and absolutist governments regiment the urban structure by establishing axes and then more axes, either parallel to each other or intersecting at right angles. Barracks, prisons, and military installations are rigidly geometrical. Citizens are not allowed to make a natural curved turning to the left or the right. They must spring round 90 degrees like marionettes. The plans of new cities are generally laid out on a grillwork. There have been exceptional cases of cities designed on hexagonal or triangular schemes, but they have never left the drawing board. New York is a chessboard, with Broadway the only diagonal. Imperial Paris is based on brutal slashes that sadistically gashed the pre-existing popular fabric of the city. Latin America was colonized with peremptory laws that imposed a priori geometrical forms on cities, whatever their natural topography might have been.

Cities, and especially capitals, are regular victims of geometrical operations. They survive only because their growth outdistances administrative and political prescriptions. Small towns, on the contrary, and particularly rural towns, are not usually geometrical, but Mafia-run settlements in rural Sicily show mercilessly rigorous geometry.

This age-old cancer, with such illustrious remissions as medieval civilization and country villages, can be extirpated only with an iron will. Architects are so influenced by inhuman and artificial geometry that it seems "natural" and "spontaneous" to them. They know no other language. And this ancestral disease is nourished by the very tools of design: T-squares, compasses, drafting machines. They serve to draw parallel lines, parallel walls, parallel rooms, parallel streets, and right-angled intersections: a world perfectly enclosed in rectangles and prisms, a world easily kept under guard by rifle or machine gun. Coffins package corpses, but being trapezoidal in form they are closer to the shape of their contents. Living men do not even have that concession. They are cynically boxed in abstract and inorganic forms.

At the end of the Middle Ages the taste for freedom from regular geometry, which coincided emblematically with the taste for liberty pure and simple, disappeared. Buildings like the Palazzo Vecchio in Florence and groups of buildings like those in Siena and Perugia look today like something from outer space. Present-day architects could not design them; the language they use will not let them. To re-educate architects, T-squares must be banned, along with compasses and all the equipment that is laid out as a function of the grammar and syntax of classical architecture.

Antigeometry and free form, and therefore asymmetry and anti-parallelism, are invariables of the modern language of architecture. They mark emancipation through dissonance.

Schoenberg wrote that dissonance should not be considered a piquant seasoning for tasteless sounds. Dissonances are logical components of a new organism that has the same vitality as the prototypes of the past. Schoenberg discovered that music freed from a tonic, or a harmonic center, was fully comprehensible and capable of evoking emotions. Tonality stands for symmetry, proportion, consonance, and geometry. Too many architects have not yet learned this lesson.

7. It would be extremely difficult to represent a medieval urban layout (for example, Siena's Piazza del Campo) using T-squares, compasses, and drafting machines. These tools are good only for boxy architecture, which can easily be represented in perspective.

III

Antiperspective Three-Dimensionality

The hecatomb took place in the early fifteenth century. It was the triumph of perspective. Architects stopped working concretely on architecture and limited themselves to designing it. The damages were enormous; they have increased through the following centuries; and they continue to proliferate with industrialized building techniques. There is probably nothing comparable in other areas of human activity. An almost unbridgeable chasm has opened up between architects and architecture. It is no wonder that quite a few architects have no idea what architecture is.

Perspective is a drawing technique for representing three-dimensional objects on a two-dimensional surface. To make the job easier, buildings were broken down into squared parts and reduced to regular prisms. An immense visual heritage of curves, asymmetric forms, swerving lines, modulations, and angles other than 90-degree was obliterated in one fell swoop. The world was turned into boxes, and the architectural "orders" were used to distinguish superimposed or juxtaposed parts of the box.

What perspective should have done was provide a means of acquiring greater awareness of three-dimensionality. Instead it rigidified three-dimensionality to such a degree that drawing it has become something mechanical and almost useless. It is a symptomatic proof of what linguists maintain: it is not we who speak a language; it is language that "speaks us." We cannot even think without a code. The perspective-based revival of classicism drastically impoverished the architectural language. Instead of inventing spaces for human life, packages were designed. With perspective, it was no longer architecture but its container that was dominant.

In theory, perspective should have provided an instrument to enhance depth. It might have expected to enrich the representation of volumes by the use of dramatic foreshortening. To that end, the corner view of a building should have become the driving force in order to pull it out of isolation and bring it into close relationship with the urban environment. Take, for instance, the Palazzo Farnese in Rome. It is a box, and it could not be anything else with the language of perspective. Yet its walls, if oblique, might have led the eye off in a series of dynamic vistas. Of course the palace's corners would have been totally different. The one facing the square should have been a clarion note, while the others would have been muted to maintain the smooth flow of streets.

Obviously, nothing of the sort was done. The Farnese Palace does not communicate any stereometric reality. It is broken up into a main façade, heavy flanks on the small side streets, and an almost independent second façade at the rear. The volume is self-contained, finished, and lacking in any interplay with its surroundings. It looks as if it had been catapulted into the square, and the only way it can be appreciated as a three-dimensional object is from the air. The façades have identical corners, the hara-kiri of perspective.

Although perspective was introduced in the name of three-dimensionality, it was usually applied to central framing, that is, two-dimensionally. Look at any Renaissance or classical street: a fissure between building walls and a procession of flat façades. Where has three-dimensionality gone? Where are the volumes? What sense was there in destroying the glorious heritage of medieval architecture, which was full of stereometric unboxed messages? Consider political and social history, and you will find an answer.

As with geometry, there would seem to be little hope of conquering the virus of perspective that has infected the body of architecture in its most intimate fiber. In this case, however, the modern code has deep roots that go right back to the fifteenth century. From Mannerism on, art has tended to overmaster perspective vision, and avant-garde movements from Impressionism

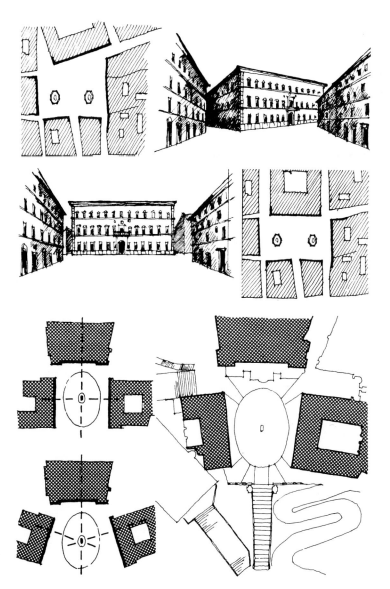

8. The three-dimensional quality of Rome's Palazzo Farnese would have been enhanced if the building had been set at an angle to the square *(above)*. Instead it appears as a two-dimensional wall *(center)*. In designing the Piazza del Campidoglio, Michelangelo rejected parallelism and traditional perspective *(below, left)* and turned the perspective trapezoid upside down *(right)*.

to *Art Informel* have speeded up the process. Architecture has lagged behind painting and sculpture: perspective has been more refractory, and it still corrupts an infinite number of buildings that are otherwise modern. A little knowledge of history is sufficient to realize that all true architects have been fighting perspective since the crisis of 1527. It is time to bring the battle to an end.

At the close of the fifteenth century there was Biagio Rossetti, the man who laid out Ferrara, "the first modern European city," as Jacob Burckhardt called it. Rossetti was not a famous artist, and that is why he understood the fundamental needs of a city, something the great architects did not grasp because they were involved with a science of optics that centered almost exclusively on single buildings. What was the discovery made by this modest craftsman who created Ferrara without even making drawings? Simply that if buildings have to belong to a context, they must not be symmetrical, self-sufficient, or finished-looking. The corner views are the keynotes that set the tone of any townscape. The rest comes by itself. In laying out the *Addizione Erculea,* the expansion of the Ferrara city area, Rossetti concentrated on the buildings at street intersections and emphasized their corners. This is the only Renaissance urban complex thought out in terms of concretely three-dimensional perspective. Yet three and a half centuries later, Baron Haussmann's Paris was conceived in terms of façades, not corners.

Michelangelo was another extraordinary man who defied central perspective. In the piazza of the Campidoglio he scorned the prevailing code, grasped the space and held it firm, violating the canons of elementary geometry. He turned a rectangle into a trapezoid that was the obverse of the perspective trapezoid, and he negated the parallelism of the two palaces flanking the square, even though they are identical. It was an incredible achievement, but its message was ignored. Michelangelo is the most famous genius in the history of art. His works are admired, measured, and copied. In Montreal there is a half-scale copy of St. Peter's. The Campidoglio is an obligatory stop on the itinerary of millions of tourists and of all cultivated architects. But how many of them, reassured by this explosive precedent, have had the courage to arrange two facing structures in nonparallel fashion?

Let us make passing reference to another overwhelming work of Michelangelo, the 1529 drawings for the fortifications of Florence. There is an unheard-of thrust of spaces within and without these walls, with embankments and ramparts driving into the surrounding landscape. There are no parallel lines in these structural profiles, twisting and turning in their function of static resistance against the double thrust of aggressive spaces. For four centuries no one has ever looked at these drawings, no one has "discovered" them, although they were perfectly well known. In terms of architectural language, of a new and revolutionary code, no use was ever made of them. Why?

Michelangelo's idiom was never formalized, so no one could speak it. What was worse, no one could understand what Michelangelo was saying. Thus, his lesson was wasted. Let me repeat, the codification of the modern language of architecture is the sine qua non if one is to speak architecture today or understand the true meaning of works of the past that have been counterfeited by classicist interpretation. This is the crux of the matter. Modern architecture coincides with the modern way of looking at the architecture of the past. One can write in a new key if one can read in a new key, and vice versa. This makes the contemporary language an instrument of formidable power even in terms of historiography.

One might object: if the classical language is the only one that has been codified, how is it possible to communicate in an anticlassical idiom? Verbal languages do not undergo such sudden and radical revolutions that you find yourself speaking one way today and another tomorrow. Furthermore, how can we establish a new architectural code on the scanty basis of a few works by some artists who, among other things, often accepted symmetry, geometrical schemes, consonance, and perspective systems? Is it not simply a pipe dream?

No. The modern language of architecture was not born suddenly in 1859 with William Morris' Red House. It does not use incomprehensible codes. Its messages are widely anticipated in Eclecticism, the Baroque, and the Renaissance itself, as we have seen, as well as the epic works of the Middle Ages, the late Roman period, Greece (the real Hellenic world, not the one defiled by Beaux-Arts hermeneutics), and as far back as the paleolithic age. Although the only formalized code is that of classicism, we are not powerless against it. The facts of history are on our side, for we know that there is not a single monument of the past

9. Once an architect has a T-square in his hand, he can no longer think architecture. He can only think about drawing it. It is the perspective language that begins "speaking him." It forces him to design in terms of boxes and prismatic orders piled on top of each other, whether they be Renaissance palaces or the grotesque "Square Colosseum" in the Fascist EUR quarter of Rome.

that obeys the classical code, and not even one Greek temple has the proportions institutionalized in the abstract idea of the "Greek temple." The so-called "classical" civilizations were not classical at all, not by a long shot. The great masters whose works provided the basis for the classical code would be the first to deny it in practice. Was Bramante classical? Was Palladio classical? Was Vignola a true classicist?

The fact that Wright, Le Corbusier, Gropius, Mies van der Rohe, Aalto, and other masters of the modern movement have sometimes adopted classical elements (usually removing them from their classical context, however) is not disturbing. The new language of architecture, which developed in dialectical opposition to Beaux-Arts idolatry, had to take the enemy's strategy into account. The relationship between the two is somewhat similar to that between the Italian language and Latin (although modern architecture is not at all derived from classicism). In the first centuries of our era, the vernacular was mixed with Latin words, and Latin was "corrupted" by vulgar terms. As time went on, Latin became progressively less Latin, and the structure of the code was vulgar. Latin came back into fashion in the fifteenth century, at the same time that perspective appeared and for similar reasons. The code of literary Latin was revived and seemed to prevail. But in that very moment it committed suicide, because the operation was antihistorical, repressive, and absurd.

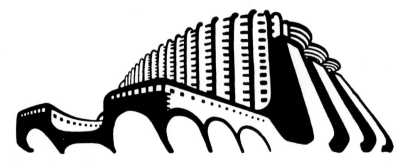

10. Erich Mendelsohn's sketch for a movie industry (1917). On the top right, three helicoidal bodies similar to the Guggenheim Museum by Frank Lloyd Wright. Mendelsohn's images do not use the Cubist four-dimensionality, but they exalt the principle of movement through corner visions and dynamic materials.

Have modern masters built some symmetrical and perspective buildings? A distinction must be made. When Gropius, Mies, and Aalto produced them, it was an act of surrender. Lacking a modern code, they weakened and regressed to the familiar womb of classicism. The same thing did not happen to Mendelsohn. His expressionism is so violent that the three-dimensional perspective block destroys any static solemnity and explodes, electrifies, and magnetizes the landscape. Where are the symmetrical buildings by Le Corbusier? Does the Villa Savoye look symmetrical? Perhaps to someone who has only glanced at it in a photograph. And Wright's works are even less symmetrical.

Finally, must we really acknowledge that perspective is one of the thousand alternatives possible? Fine, so long as it is chosen out of a thousand possibilities, after the advantages of the other nine hundred and ninety-nine have been examined, and not a priori.

IV

The Syntax of Four-dimensional Decomposition

De Stijl theory, the only coherent attempt to draw up a code for modern architecture, offered a rigorous procedure that could be applied generally. If the problem is to get rid of the perspective block, the first thing to do is eliminate the third dimension by decomposing the box, breaking it up into panels. No more closed volumes. What happens to a room? It is no longer a cubic void. There are six plans: the ceiling, four walls, and the floor. Separate the joinings, keeping the planes free; then light will penetrate even the darkest corners of the room, and its space will take on new life. A simple operation no one had thought of before, yet it was a decisive step on the way to architectural emancipation. The interior space is still somewhat cubical, but it looks completely different with this sort of lighting.

Let us follow this line of inquiry. Once the plans are separate and independent, they can be extended beyond the perimeter of the old box and spread out, go up or down, and reach beyond the limits that used to cut off the interior from the exterior. House and city can be transformed, Mondrian fashion, into a panorama of blue, yellow, red, white, and black panels. Once the box has been dismembered, the planes no longer form closed volumes, containers of finite spaces. Instead the rooms become fluid and join up and flow in a moving continuum. The static quality of classicism is replaced by a dynamic vision, with the element of time added or, if you will, with a fourth dimension.

There was enough in De Stijl theory to nourish the language of architecture for decades. It would have been an easy step from planes to curved and wavy surfaces and free forms, with a wealth

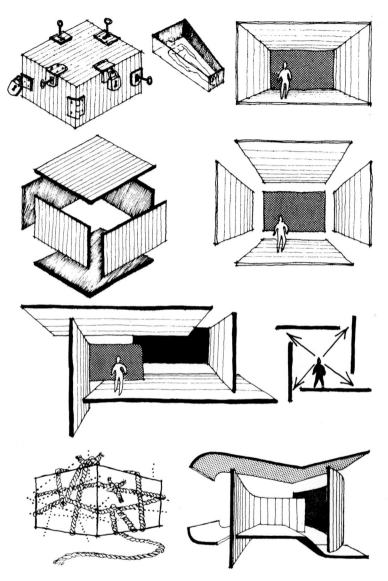

11. The box encloses, confining one like a coffin *(above)*. But if we separate the box's six planes, we have performed the revolutionary act of modern architecture *(second row)*. The panels can be lengthened or shortened to vary the light in fluid spaces *(third row)*. Once the box has been broken up, the spaces can perform their functions in total freedom *(below)*.

of alternative passages from space to space. But architects did not understand this neoplastic code, and so they abandoned it without having fully explored its possibilities.

Nevertheless, decomposition remains a substantial invariable of the modern idiom. In the Bauhaus complex in Dessau, for example, Gropius broke up the volume into three distinct units: the dormitory, the school, and the workshop. Programmatically dissonant blocks are thus linked together in defiance of perspective. There is no vantage point from which you can grasp the whole. You have to walk around. Hence movement, hence time. It is still, as always, a question of inventorying functions. Once the compact box is destroyed, the functional components can be distinguished, and their messages become more specific and direct. Harmonic connections are rejected. The passages between the three blocks look crude and brutal to emphasize their dissonance.

Gropius only half understood what De Stijl was up to, and he did not break up volumes into panels. Other architects only half understood what had been done at the Bauhaus. The practice of breaking up volumes into smaller functional units was widely adopted, especially in school buildings, where it is easy to separate the classroom block from the gymnasium and the offices. But generally there is an attempt to "harmonize" the three units, to make them reciprocally "proportional" and to link them up with "assonant" transitions—in short, to classicize the anticlassical. How can one explain that dissonance is as fundamental to modern architecture as it is to modern music? It is what gives forms, words, and sounds their specific meaning and makes expressive the inventory of functions. Yet no sooner do architects get the wrapping off than they start putting it back on again. When the classroom block, the gymnasium, and the office body are "composed" harmoniously, we are back with perspective vision again, with a privileged vantage point.

The mania of proportion is another tumor that needs to be cut out. What is proportion? It is a device to establish a binding relationship between heterogeneous parts of a building. It is a neurotic longing for "synthesis," preferably a priori. But if the parts are different and carry specific messages, why unify them

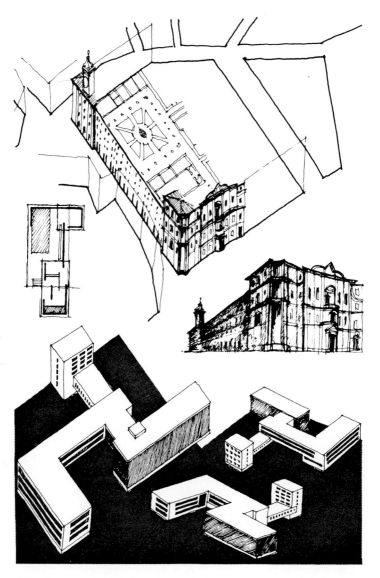

12. The decomposition of the volume block into functional prisms was carried out in the Monastery of San Filippo Neri in Rome, designed by Francesco Borromini *(above)*, and in Walter Gropius' Bauhaus at Dessau *(below)*. Ludwig Mies van der Rohe, in Barcelona, broke the volume up into free panels *(left, center)*.

through proportion and reduce the number of messages to one? Fear of freedom, of growth, and therefore of life. Any time you see a "proportioned" building, beware! Proportion freezes the vital process and masks falsity and waste.

Mies van der Rohe is perhaps the outstanding exponent of De Stijl. His German Pavilion at the Barcelona Exposition of 1929 is a masterpiece of this architectural trend. It consists of panels in travertine and marble, glass sheets, water surfaces, horizontal and vertical planes that shatter the immobility of closed spaces, break through volumes, and give direction to exterior vistas. This pavilion was only a beginning, with all its planes at right angles to each other. The system could have been enriched by getting away from the right angle and moving along inclined planes. But the pavilion was the beginning and the end. Four-dimensional decomposition became a plaything, a mindless exercise suitable for designing balconies, awnings, and some furnishings.

For clarity's sake, let us digress for a moment. The modern code is applicable in any situation, on any scale, from a chair to a highway cluster, from a spoon to a city. An architect should not refuse any challenge. If he waits for the ideal commission before "speaking" correctly, he has already given up his profession. Take a room, for example, even the most traditional and anachronistic one. Let us start by painting its surfaces six different colors: yellow, red, blue, white, black, and another color for the floor. Is it still the same room? Now let us change the color arrangement: make the ceiling black, and the walls blue, red, white, and yellow. The dark ceiling pressing down will make the room seem broader. If you want more light, the wall facing the window will be white or yellow. If you want less light, that wall can be painted blue or red, or even black. And let us paint the rectangular areas over windows and doors right up to the ceiling, so that they become sections of the wall instead of holes. And why not use lines? All it takes is a diagonal stroke to dynamize a surface. Nowadays supergraphic design is within everybody's reach.

One might object that these are cosmetic operations. Certainly they are, but cosmetics can be a corrective and a protest. The classical code is shot through with cosmetic expedients, from useless colonnades to fake windows. The modern code uses cosmetics as a provocation, to point out the burning need for a new treatment of space.

Moreover, modern cosmetics are neither costly nor wasteful, while the old cosmetics—what with symmetry, proportion, and marble facing—are prohibitively expensive. Consider the nineteenth-century Palazzo della Regina Margherita on the Via Veneto in Rome. Conceived in classical terms, it needed a majestic "fullness" on top, to make the cornice dominant. So an entire floor was built for this sole purpose, a floor that could not be lived in because there were no windows. Isn't that disgraceful? After World War II, the Americans bought the building for the United States Embassy. They found that there was a top floor and wanted to put it to use, so they cut a series of small windows in the cornice. Double madness: a "royal" embassy with affectations of efficiency. The modern language of architecture could not build or even design such a building, much less something like the Victor Emmanuel Monument. The modern language was born with social, psychological, and human aims, and it abhors pompous display and superstructures. Classical architecture is very expensive because it is symbolic. It must assert itself and suffocate the citizen.

The method of decomposition is an invariable. The seventh invariable, the principle of reintegration, means something only if it is the result of prior decomposition. Otherwise it is not reintegration but merely a priori classical integration.

The fourth invariable was not a 1917 discovery of the Dutch De Stijl group. Consider the San Filippo Neri Monastery in Rome. Borromini designed this enormous block in the seventeenth century. He broke it up into sections that are functional in terms of both interior spaces and cityscape. It has a concave front that pulls in the outside world. To the left is a supreme corner, perhaps the most highly elaborated angle in the history of architecture, leading seductively into a small side street. Facing onto it is a long opaque wall with almost casual, dissonant windows. But at the end of the street the Piazza dell'Orologio seems to urge the building to send up its tower and tease the sky with linear, wrought-iron arabesques. Truly, the "modern" structures of the past overshadow the classical ones. Life has always decomposed, articulated, added, or subtracted. Delacroix said that a straight line does not exist. Scientists tell us that symmetry is not a law of nature. Likewise, classicism does not exist in architecture, only in Beaux-Arts manuals and buildings that are copied out of them.

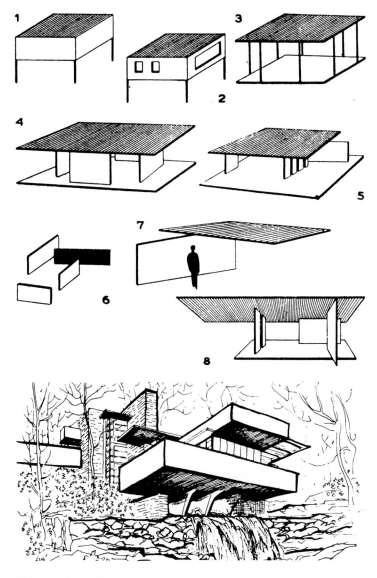

13. Eight sketches to illustrate a lecture by Frank Lloyd Wright on the involvement of every architectural element in the structural scheme. *Below:* the Kaufmann House, Falling Water, at Bear Run, Pennsylvania (1936–39), which incorporates all seven invariables of the modern language of architecture.

V

Cantilever, Shell, and Membrane Structures

"Now I shall try to show you why organic architecture is the architecture of democratic freedom. . . . Here—say—is your box: big hole in the box, little ones if you wish—of course. What you see of it now is this square package of containment. You see? Something not fit for our liberal profession of democratic government, a thing essentially anti-individual. . . . I knew enough of engineering to know that the outer angles of a box were not where its most economical support would be. . . . No, a certain distance in each way from each corner is where the economic support of a box-building is invariably to be found. You see? Now, when you put support at those points you have created a short cantileverage to the corners that lessens actual spans and sets the corner free or open for whatever distance you choose. The corners disappear altogether if you choose to let space come in there, or let it go out. Instead of post and beam construction, the usual box building, you now have a new sense of building construction by way of the cantilever and continuity. Both are new structural elements as they now enter architecture. But all you see of this radical liberation of space all over the world today, is the corner window. But, in this simple change of thought lies the essential of the architectural change from box to free plan and the new reality that is *space* instead of matter. . . . Let's go on. These unattached side walls become something independent, no longer enclosing walls. They're separate supporting screens, any one of which may be shortened, or extended or perforated, or occasionally eliminated. . . . freedom where before imprisonment existed. You can perfect a figure of freedom with these

39

four screens; in any case, enclosure as a box is gone. . . . To go further: if this liberation works in the horizontal plane why won't it work in the vertical plane? No one has looked through the box at the sky up there at the upper angle, have they? Why not? Because the box always had a cornice at the top. . . . Now . . . you catch no sense of enclosure whatever at any angle, top or sides. . . . Space may now go out or come in where life is being lived, space as a component of it" (Frank Lloyd Wright, *An American Architecture,* ed. Edgar Kaufman [New York: Horizon Press, 1955], pp. 76–78). Wright anticipated De Stijl syntax and got to the heart of the problem by way of analyzing structures.

It is elementary reasoning to place the supports a certain distance in from the corners. Even a child can understand it. But how many architects can? Look around you. Millions of supports are put up at the corners, cagelike structures hemming in space. And what about engineers? With few exceptions, they are victims of classical prejudices and make things symmetrical and proportionate. Indeed, the history of engineering is brimful of compromise. A striking example is the Eiffel Tower in Paris. The four large arches at its base look as if they were meant to support the structure, but they are false. The famous French engineer could not face the "scandal" of building the tower in its true structural form, with four shafts meeting at the top. He had to respect classical "static vision," even denying reality. Thus he installed a large heavy beam, serving no purpose, on all four sides and hung the arches on them. The arches are supported, but they look as if they were doing the supporting. Classicists were satisfied with this typically wasteful act.

The codification of the modern language of architecture implies that engineers as well as architects must shuck the chains of classicism and bring to an end the long conflict between technique and expression, which must be used together in a creative fashion.

Take a prestigious international figure like Pier Luigi Nervi. He produced a masterpiece in the Orbetello hangars, with their magnificent enclosed space, arching volumes, and corner elements that project the structure into the landscape. His Turin Exhibition Hall had splendid modules, but they are repeated in the traditional way and could not be carried through to the end walls. To finish

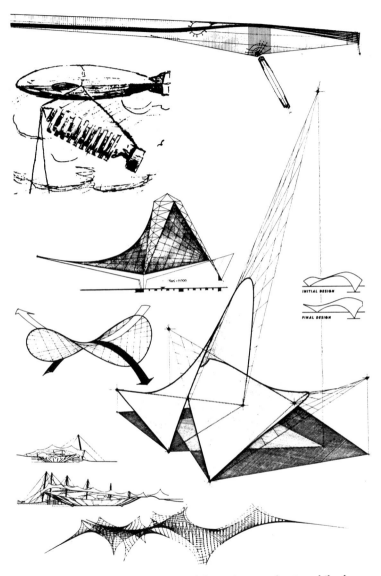

14. Modern structures. *Above:* section of the underground automobile showroom in Turin, by Riccardo Morandi; a dirigible towing a skyscraper, by Buckminster Fuller. *Center:* three hyperbolic paraboloids, by Felix Candela; *right:* skin membranes, by Eduardo Torroja. *Below:* Frei Otto's membranes.

them off, an awful apse was built with pseudostructural decorative elements. Nervi's Palazzo del Lavoro in Turin is a thankless large box, with reinforced concrete columns complete with fluting and steel capitals. All it would take to turn it into an Egyptian temple are colossal statues of pharaohs. To comment on his papal audience hall in the Vatican would be superfluous. And the most that can be said of that round cake, the Palazzo dello Sport in Rome, is that it is right at home in the Fascist EUR complex designed by Marcello Piacentini, the Italian Albert Speer. The Palazzetto dello Sport in Viale Tiziano is certainly better, but what is that circle of fork-shaped elements that supports the dome? A circular ring of prestressed reinforced concrete, the real structural link of the whole organism, is hidden underground. And what is one to think of this mania for domes? The symbolism of the dome is associated with godhead, idols, absolute monarchies, temple shrines, and dictatorial states. Psychologically, the dome involves security or its counterfeit because it is the classic form par excellence, completely closed and symmetrical. Nervi did not draw inspiration from the anticlassical domes of Hagia Sophia in Istanbul or Santa Maria del Fiore in Florence, but from the Pantheon, and he executed a series of tours de force to reduce the thickness of the shell. Where the Pantheon piles up matter, Nervi throws open a row of windows. Nevertheless, the space is still blocked, and there is no interplay with the world outside. The security to be found in the shadow of classical idols is simply fear decked out in fancy trappings.

What happened to Nervi after the Orbetello hangars? Did his creative streak run dry? Suffice it to look at the Burgo paper plant in Mantua and countless details of the buildings mentioned above to see that it did not. The reason is simpler and much more alarming. When Nervi speaks architecture, he speaks Latin, the classical code that exhausts most structural engineers. How many are immune from it? Riccardo Morandi for one, especially in his underground automobile showroom in Turin; Buckminster Fuller, with his air-transportable geodesic domes and extremely lightweight skyscrapers; Eduardo Torroja, with his Madrid Racecourse vaults; Félix Candela with his hyperbolic paraboloids; Frei Otto with his transparent tensilstructures; and quite a few young men who are slowly sloughing off the classical code, particularly in their shell and membrane, or plastic and compressed air, coverings. Architecture and engineering come together in these "tents," where space forms, and is formed by, the structures.

The structural invariable of the modern idiom is less concerned with cantilevers, membranes, and shells than it is with involving all the architectural elements in a symphony of static forces. It is well known that a structure's efficiency depends on its form and the tension of its curves. But how many people take this principle into consideration? In an ordinary balcony, it is only the slab that does the structural work, not the railing or parapet; hence, waste.

But look at the astonishing Falling Water house. The cantilevered terrace seemed so precarious to the workmen that they refused to take down the scaffolding for fear that the whole thing would collapse. Wright pulled down the scaffolding himself. Even in structural engineering he spoke the modern language. He proved his worth in works that "sensible" people and academicians considered mad and suicidal.

In the building field, science is still in an antediluvian slumber. Enormous transatlantic liners can float on water, while city buildings are made inordinately heavy just to stand on the ground. A considerable patrimony of structural experiences is not drawing interest. Sergio Musmeci said: "The lack of technological foresight is responsible for the present crisis in architecture and is keeping it from becoming truly modern. History must be brought up to date by making a leap out of the past and into the future. The problem of creating forms for the future can be postponed no longer."

15. Wavy surface design by the computer of the Aerospace Division of the Boeing Company. This shape would be almost impossible to design with the architect's traditional tools: T-square, compasses, drafting machines. Computers can suggest new forms to enrich the lexicon, grammar, and syntax of architecture.

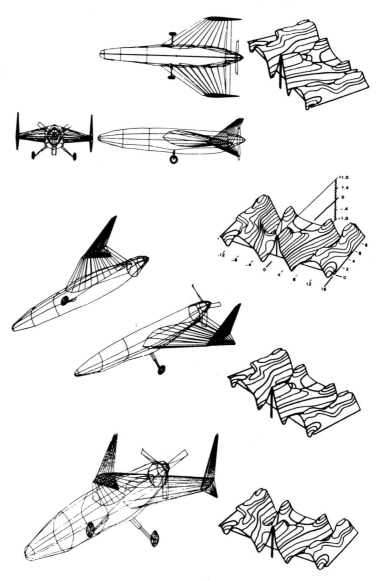

16. Drawings produced by the computer of the Airplane Division of the Boeing Company. They show how to depict the same object from different points of view by using computer-directed simulators. With this sort of technical support, imaginative architectural designs can be verified at once from all sides.

Is this utopian? Not at all. It is simply an appeal to use electronic computers to solve structural and technological problems, including service installations, with a speed and exactitude that were unattainable before. Computers are becoming more and more popular. In a few years perhaps the structural engineer as we know him, immersed in mysterious but rough calculations, will disappear. We will have slender, lightweight, prefabricated, and portable buildings. We may no longer "go to work" and "come home." Perhaps we shall just press a button, and home or office, suspended from a helicopter, may come to us, settling down wherever we like.

The technological revolution coincides with the revolution in architectural language. Computers make it possible to simulate reality, not in the unilateral way perspective drawing does, but in all its visual and behavioral aspects. We can check the space of a room, its size, light, heating, and fluency. The simulator will instantly draw plans, sections, elevations; it will walk us through a building or a city; and it will be possible to compare an infinite number of alternate solutions. Obviously it will not guarantee that architects speak the modern language, but it will offer them the possibility of doing so, a possibility that has hitherto been limited by the very instruments of design, T-squares and compasses. What is more, computers will make the design

17. The architect of the future (cartoon in *AIA Journal*). He describes his idea to a secretary, who feeds the information to a computer. The machine goes to work, and a robot builds the three-dimensional structure.

process democratic. The client will be able to follow the development of his house step by step. He will "see" it and "live" it before it is built. He will be able to make choices and change the house. The breach that has separated the architect from architecture, at least since the Renaissance, will finally be closed, as will the breach between space and its structural shell.

VI

Space in Time

The history of architecture is marked by chances missed, giant steps forward, and long falls backward. Michelangelo took a giant step forward; everyone praised him, but no one followed where he led. Borromini leaped forward; he was ostracized during his lifetime and dismissed after his death. Constructivism marked a major advance after the October Revolution, but Stalin, good classicist that he was, froze the movement. Wright burst forth, but where are the traces of his work in our present panorama?

It is easy to understand why so many give up the battle. It is hard to escape from the academic womb. At best, compromise is achieved, and that is even worse. An architect who said, "I want to speak ancient Greek" would probably be considered mad, but he would actually be less demented than those who unconsciously speak an ungrammatical version of ancient Greek, ignorant of its vocabulary and syntax. Only one architect of our time sought and found architecture in ancient Greece. And he discovered it for himself, without the blinders of the Beaux-Arts school. That man was Charles-Edouard Jeanneret, who changed his name to Le Corbusier after his baptism in Greek waters. The only way to speak ancient Greek would be to formulate the invariables of the language: antiperspective, no alignment or parallelism of volumes, ban on symmetry (in the name of the Propylaea), and a veto on classicism (in the name of the Erechtheum). Are these not the invariables of modern architecture? Of course, and the only way to get free of perspective conditioning is to go back to preperspective civilizations, usually to the Middle Ages but in Le Corbusier's case to Greece. Take Hadrian's Villa in Tivoli,

47

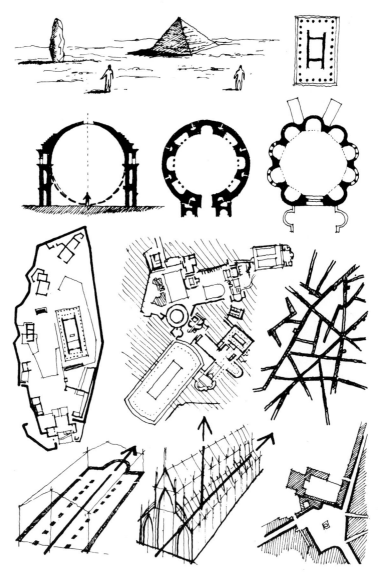

18. Closed spaces: a menhir, a pyramid, and a Greek temple *(above)*. Static interior spaces: the Pantheon and the Temple of Minerva Medica in Rome *(second row)*. Spaces to move through: the Acropolis, Athens; Hadrian's Villa, Tivoli; catacombs, Rome *(third row)*. Paleo-Christian one-directional movement; Gothic two-directional movement; Baroque movement, Piazza del Quirinale, Rome *(below)*.

for example. Does it speak the classical language or something diametrically opposite, with its hinged blocks swinging around and reaching out to the landscape? The idea of "the classical world" is a meaningless abstraction. Paradoxical as it may seem, "classical" civilization was almost totally anticlassical.

Space in time is the summary of the problem in a nutshell. It took man thousands of years to master architectural space. The time element in architecture was experienced for only a short and exceptional period, that of the catacombs. It will take centuries, perhaps thousands of years, for man to master the dynamic principle of space in time.

The only way to become modern is by reliving the stages of past history inside oneself. Before the Pantheon there were no interior spaces created by man. There were empty, unfilled voids and left-over, negative cavities. Primitive man was afraid of space. His monument was the menhir, an upright "long stone," a "fullness" in the endless wastes. The ancient East produced a number of solids, like the pyramids and temples with hypostyle halls, where space was driven out by enormous columns. The Greek temple humanized volume, but it continued to ignore space. The idea of using nontactile reality as an architectural instrument was first put into practice in the Pantheon. But its space is timid, hemmed in by gigantic walls and lacking contact with the outside. It is lighted only by a single oculus at the top, which heightens the chiaroscuro of the coffered dome and confirms that this is solid heavy matter. A few centuries went by before man was ready for the interplay of inner spaces and outside landscape. This did not happen until late antiquity, with the so-called Temple of Minerva Medica in Rome. And the idea of continuous flow between inner and outer space was only made concrete a thousand years later, in the Gothic cathedrals.

There was a period in which the physical world was considered a place of damnation, and a life after death was hypothesized. Man lived for the hereafter and scorned terrestrial values. Space was repressed. Endless hypogeal tunnels for the dead were dug beneath the static, theatrically monumental architecture of ancient Rome. The element of time thus came into its own with the birth of this architecture-to-move-through. The catacombs were only moved through, they did not lead anywhere. It was the Biblical approach in a metaphysical and transcendental key, an architecture of suicide. This was a short-lived experience in history. As the Church became wordly, it came to terms with administrative and political authority. The element of time encountered the Greco-Roman sense of space. Movement was preserved along the length of the Christian basilica, from narthex to apse, but columns and walls on both sides of the nave were organized in classical fashion, with a single axial motion line. Only in the Gothic cathedral was something more complex achieved, in the contrast between two lines of motion: the length of the church, which can be moved through physically; and a vertical course marking an ideal passage heavenward.

The time element was constricted in the Renaissance. Pure space prevailed again, along with the self-sufficient object and the central-plan building. The furious battle over St. Peter's Basilica in Rome was concerned with stasis and movement, Reformation and Counter Reformation. Michelangelo's scheme was butchered to make room for a theatrical plan. Borromini revived Michelangelo's idea in the church of Sant'Agnese in the Piazza Navona, and in Sant'Ivo alla Sapienza he showed that the impossible was possible, that a centralized space could be truly dynamic. His triumphant shout died out without an echo.

The Biblical concept of life implies movement and change. The Greco-Roman concept involves static space. The Christian Church struck a dubious balance between the two. There was multidirectional movement in the plan of Pope Sixtus' Rome and in the layout of Baroque cities. Then came the neoclassical freeze.

The sixth invariable of the modern language is space in time, space that is truly lived in, ready to act and be acted on. When the first five invariables are caught up by space in time, they acquire new substance. Functional listing is the premise. Asymmetry and dissonance are indispensable features, because a symmetrical building makes movement useless; all you can do is stand still and look at it. Antiperspective is another consequence of space in time, because it means constantly changing the viewing point. Decomposition and projecting structures are instruments

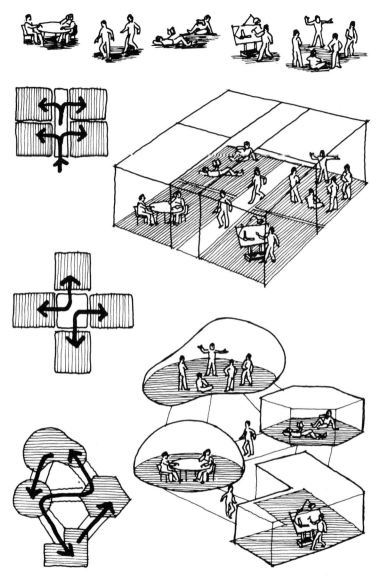

19. Architecture without buildings. The architect must study human functions without worrying about how to box them in *(above)*. He must avoid forcing them into single boxes or series of regular prisms *(center)*. The modern language of architecture adapts spaces to human functions and movements *(below)*.

for adding the time element to architecture. They break up the box and bite its corners.

How can time be introduced into space? One way was pointed out by Louis Kahn. He distinguished between spaces to move through and spaces created for "arrivals" at the end of movement. Anyone who conceives of a corridor with parallel walls, that is as a static prism, does not know the first thing about architecture. Even the arrival spaces—living room, study, or bedroom—should not be totally static. They must foster human communication, intellectual tension, or waking after sleep. Life is always full of happenings. The dynamism of living needs to be mediated but not reduced to zero. A room is entered, crossed, and left, and all this movement should be considered and provided for in design. What is the "free plan," the principle of flexibility, moving partitions, and fluidity from space to space? It is another way of expressing space in time and time in space. The volume of Villa Savoye, in Poissy, is slashed from ground to roof garden by a ramp that is visible throughout the house. Le Corbusier called it *promenade architecturale,* architecture to walk through.

Staircases are certainly moved through, but too many of them are caged in vertical tubes. In the Swiss Pavilion of the University of Paris, the staircases emerge from the volume and a "free-hand" curved wall caresses them. A more advanced example is the staircases in Aalto's dormitories at the Massachusetts Institute of Technology in Cambridge, which are continuous with the corridors in order to form serpentine volumes and spaces. And what about the famous building that is all passageway and ramp? The Guggenheim Museum in New York is that kind of structure, an extrovert helical *promenade.*

Norris Kelly Smith maintains that Wright introduced Biblical thought into the field of architecture for the first time, after two thousand years of domination by Greco-Roman concepts. It was easier for Wright to escape from classicism because he turned down a Beaux-Arts education. He hated big cities, bureaucratic institutions, authority, and power, and kept intact the proud individualism of the pioneers. At Taliesin, Wisconsin, and Taliesin West, Arizona, he lived close to nature and experienced and studied time. How, indeed, could you think of building a house over a waterfall if you did not have a vivid sense of fluid motion? In the Guggenheim Museum a glass strip was wound around the spiral, so that paintings and sculptures could receive a mixture of natural and artificial light. The time element marks the transition from the city to the museum inside and vice versa. The lighting of the interior space was to change tone every hour all year round.

Where in architecture can time be introduced? Everywhere. How can it be done? In countless ways. Take floors, for example. Does it make sense to have the same kind of floor surface in the hallway, the living room, the bathroom, the study, and the bedroom? Should movement and kinetic experience be the same in rooms with such different functions? Where could such an inane rule have come from? Classicism, of course. What basis could it have? Certainly not the so-called classical period, which reveals a remarkable sense of movement: the Athenian Acropolis is built on rough rocky terrain, kept that way in order to impose slow, architecturally calculated motion. Every space should have different flooring—hard, soft, gravelly, smooth or rough, oblique, any kind as long as it is thought out. Einstein says that an event is localized not only in time but also in space. This revolutionary idea has yet to be assimilated by architecture. What it means is the following invariable: open design that is constantly in process, invested with time consciousness, and unfinished.

20. Frank Lloyd Wright, from listing to reintegration. *Above:* three-dimensional drawing for the Martin and Barton Houses in Buffalo, New York (1903–4); the single units are functionally articulated. *Below:* the Guggenheim Museum, New York (1946–59); a spiral turning outward to the city.

VII

Reintegration of Building, City, and Landscape

If listing functions is the first invariable of the modern code of architecture, then reintegration is logically the last one. The five invariables in between could be increased in number by passing from the elementary level to an exhaustive analysis of the lexicon, grammar, and syntax of architecture.

Inventorying functions breaks up the box, lists elements without classifying them, and gives concrete new meaning to the individual messages that classicism drowned in "orders" and sequences of proportions. The successive invariables reinforce the listing operation by discarding the inviolable taboos of symmetry, assonance, geometry, perspective, compact volumes, structural corners, and space with no time component. Thus they also foster a reintegration of the functions that have been listed. The "free plan" by itself is a step on the road to reintegration, because it postulates maximum communication and flow between rooms and thereby unifies them. But this is not synthesis in the classic, a priori sense. It is just the opposite, a matter of dynamic unity that creates a movement and shapes space to time. True, you move physically even in a classical building, but man always has the impression of being out of place and incongruous there. Those spaces were designed not for him, but for motionless statues, and they are as formal as tombs.

Adolf Loos explored the principle of vertical reintegration in his Raumplan (an interlocking construct of spatial areas of different heights) and enlarged the surface available for living, thereby economizing and increasing artistic values. There is no reason why the service area or the sleeping area cannot be lower than

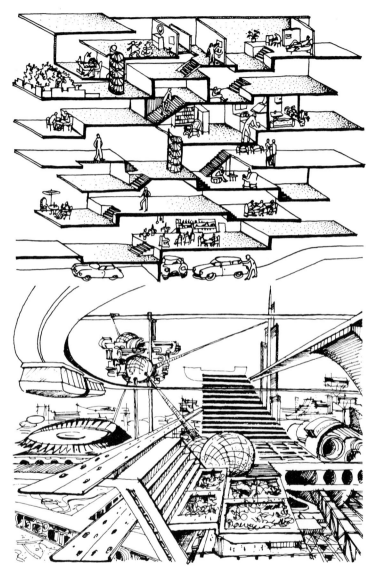

21. Raumplan and reintegration. *Above:* the staggered levels break up the mechanical superimposition of floors and provide each room with the functionally correct height, without waste. *Below:* an urban plan that brings collective and residential structures into close contact with streets, parks, and transportation systems, taking advantage of several levels.

the living room. And we can use the differences in height to create other usable spaces that are intimate, interesting, and accessible in a few steps. For an example of the opposite principle, take a symbol of Fascism, the Palazzo Littorio in Rome, completed after the war as the seat of the Ministry of Foreign Affairs. The bathroom ceilings are over twenty feet high, the same height as those of the assembly halls. These imperial toilets are fit for fairytale giants or Duces on fifteen-foot stilts. Instead, they are used by little men who look sadly out of place there. They are another example of classicist schizophrenia.

Our aim is horizontal and vertical reintegration, with passages in any direction, not squared off at right angles but curving, oblique, and inclined. This principle goes well beyond the single object and integrally links the building to the city. When the volume has been broken up into planes and reassembled in four-dimensional fashion, the traditional façade disappears, together with the distinction between interior and exterior spaces and between architecture and town planning. The fusion of city and building leads to "urbatecture." No more building blocks alternating with empty blocks for streets and plazas. Once the old weave is unraveled, the landscape can be reintegrated. And when the traditional dichotomy of city and countryside is abolished, urbatecture can spread into whole territories, while nature penetrates the metropolitan fabric. Thus continuity will be established between city and region, instead of overcrowded, polluted, chaotic, and homicidal urban communities on the one hand and desolate, uncultivated countryside on the other.

Is this utopian? Only in so far as it is still just an aspiration. If it becomes a spoken language in design, in furnishings, in your own room, in buildings of any size, in a city, and in its region, it will acquire an overwhelming force. Architects and people interested in the human habitat will have at their disposal a revolutionary weapon, one that is actually explosive by virtue of architecture. If we really speak the modern architectural language, there are two possibilities facing us. Either we will be allowed to express ourselves freely, or we will have to demolish the obstacles that prevent us from doing so, we will have to fight censorship. Does real-estate speculation gag free speech? Then we must combat

22. John Johansen, from listing to reintegration. The Mummers Theater, Oklahoma City. The elements are laid out on the ground ("place it"). Then comes structure ("support it"), followed by traffic tubes ("connect it"). Thus a city-and-building object, fully opened to its surroundings, is achieved.

it with a vigor that is commensurate with the importance of urba-
tectural language. But our cause will be weakened if, once the
use of land has been collectivized, nothing changes in terms of
architectural censorship, as was the case in Soviet Russia.

Obviously this last invariable has functional consequences too.
After having listed and decomposed the functions of buildings,
cities, and territories, we must rethink their relationships. Why
should a school be a self-contained structure instead of being
one with the social center, the local administrative offices, factories, professional studios, and residences? Is it right to separate
residential from recreational and commercial areas? Should we
not rather promote an interplay of functions? Take the case of
universities, which used to consist of several independent facul-
ties, each with its own classrooms, auditorium, and library. Inter-
disciplinary education has started breaking through this kind of
isolationism. Will universities continue to move outside the city,
like the traditional English and American campuses, or will they
be localized throughout the residential and working areas?

Streets must also be reintegrated. On several floors of the Unité
d'Habitation in Marseilles, Le Corbusier inserted stores, thus
reintegrating business and residence. He called these corridors
rues, veritable indoor streets. Why cannot streets run at the same
height as the tenth or fiftieth floor of the buildings, floating between skyscrapers and structuring the sky? Countless utopian
designs offer urban images of this kind, and a number of architectural works foreshadow them in concrete fashion.

The offices of the Ford Foundation in New York look out onto
an inner covered park. A building on the Via Romagna in Rome
reintegrates commercial, administrative, and residential functions
by having stores, offices, and villas piled on top of each other.
The Mummers Theater in Oklahoma City is a construct of heterogeneous fragments, scrap metal, automobile wrecks, and tubes—
action architecture, as John Johansen's sketches clearly show.
Montreal's Habitat '67 is a cluster of cells that link up architectural
and urban spaces with streets on all levels. This structure could
be enlarged to accommodate schools, hospitals, plazas, gardens,
and parks; the sort of do-it-yourself architecture, flowing and
free from geometry, that Louis Kahn envisaged in his sketch.

Unless the population problem is to be solved by nuclear war, macrostructures are urgently needed, but not terrifying macrostructures. On the contrary, they should be human, comfortable, and life-enhancing, with exciting spaces for collective activities and intimate spaces for privacy.

Reintegration of city and region implies a dialogue between

23. Assembly of residential units at Habitat '67, Montreal, by Moshe Safdie. *Above:* two cartoons on Habitat, by Ting and Daigneault. *Below:* a sketch by Louis Kahn; he objected to the boxlike shapes of Safdie's units and suggested that they be assembled freely, like leaves on a tree.

architecture and its natural environment. Psychoanalysis and anthropology teach and warn us that man has lost some essential values in his rise to civilization: the sense of the unity of space and time, the freedom of nomadic life, the joy of aimless wandering through unlimited horizons. We can and must recover these values. The hippy communes and the revolt of the young against consumer society, polluted cities, and repressive institutions are symptoms of the urgent need to wipe the cultural slate clean. But one makes a new start by moving forward, providing concrete alternatives and using the modern language that can express them. Otherwise one is mired in mere romantic protest, blocked at zero degrees.

Again, let us think of some simple cases that can be easily verified. The reader can make his own extrapolations on the urban and territorial scale. What does reintegrating architecture and nature mean? Walk into a cave or a natural grotto. It may once have been the refuge for prehistoric man. You can feel the earth beneath your feet, and you like the feeling. This sense of physical pleasure has been lost on our asphalt streets and smooth sidewalks. The roof of the cave is not squared off at the sides; it is continuous with the curving rough walls and runs right into the earth floor. When light strikes the rocky masses or glances over the vault of the cave, it creates stunning magical effects that change hour after hour. And think about grottoes by the sea, where the light picks up the color of the depths as it is reflected by the water surface. The light moves with the waves, records the sky, whether cloudy or calm, and communicates the shifting of the winds. All these lost values can be rediscovered through the modern language of architecture. In the Massachusetts Institute of Technology chapel, Eero Saarinen illuminated the space with a tremulous light reverberating off water. Despite controversial opinions about its success, this solution is indicative of what can be done. The reintegration of architecture and nature must be carried out in a scientific, not a romantic way, on the basis of anthropological, sociological, and psychoanalytical research. The modern code demands it.

From listing functions to reintegration, there are seven invariables that bear witness against idolatry, dogma, conventions, set

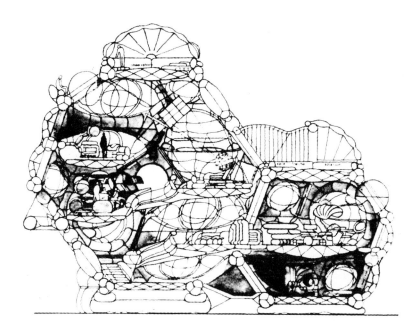

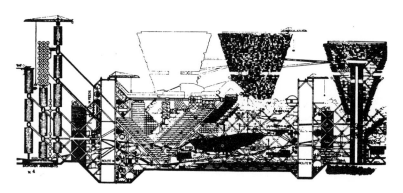

24. *Above:* a community building with pneumatic structures that attempt to recover the tactile and figural values of prehistoric caves, designed by J. P. Jungmann of the French Utopie group. *Below:* a new integrated city, with macrostructures and connecting tubes, designed by the British Archigram group.

phrases, commonplaces, humanistic imprecision, and repressive-ness, in whatever conscious or unconscious form these may ap-pear. The new language "speaks us" straight out, without mystical overtones, not only for the present and the future but all the way back to prehistory. To borrow from Arnold Schoenberg, the modern language brings together the idea of Moses and the word of Aaron.

Conclusion: Unfinished Architecture and Kitsch

It is worth comparing two modern theses, one expressed in the iconoclastic appeal of Friedrich Hundertwasser and the other in the mournful reflections of Saul Bellow's Mr. Sammler.

Hundertwasser says in his "Manifesto for the Boycotting of Architecture": "Every man has the right to build the way he wants. Architecture today is censored the same way painting is in the Soviet Union. Everybody should be entitled to build his own four walls and be responsible for them. Present-day architecture is criminally sterile. The reason is that building stops when the client enters his residence, yet that is precisely when it should begin, and grow like skin on a human organism." Hence, to the stake with architects; their job and privileges should be turned over to the consumers, to the people.

Mr. Sammler is much more skeptical about spontaneous creativity: "Then: a crazy species? Yes, perhaps. Though madness is also a masquerade, the project of a deeper reason. . . . And what to do? In the matter of histrionics, see, for instance, what that furious world-boiler Marx had done, insisting that revolutions were made in historical costume, the Cromwellians as Old Testament prophets, the French in 1789 dressed in Roman outfits. But the proletariat, he said, he declared, he affirmed, would make the first nonimitative revolution. It would not need the drug of historical recollection. From sheer ignorance, knowing no models, it would simply do the thing pure. He was as giddy as the rest about originality. And only the working class was original. Thus history would get away from mere poetry. Then the life of humankind would clear itself of copying. It would be free from Art.

Oh, no. No, no, not so, thought Sammler. Instead, Art increased, and a sort of chaos." Stalin's proletarian society copied the architecture of autocracy and despotism, and people who practiced confrontation politics "were obviously derivative. And of what— of Paiutes, of Fidel Castro? No, of Hollywood extras. Acting mythic. . . . Better, thought Sammler, to accept the inevitability of imitation and then to imitate good things. . . . Greatness without models? Inconceivable. . . . Make peace therefore with intermediacy and representation. But choose higher representations. Otherwise the individual must be the failure he now sees and knows himself to be. Mr. Sammler, sorry for all, and sore at heart" (*Mr. Sammler's Planet* [New York: Viking, 1970], pp. 148– 49).

Mr. Sammler is right, an architectural code is needed. But the liberating force of the modern language of architecture is oriented toward Hundertwasser's objectives. It teaches one to desanctify the canons and precepts of the Enlightenment for the sake of more concrete choices. The seven invariables all refer to specific models, from William Morris' Red House to the masterpieces of Wright, Le Corbusier, Gropius, Mies, Aalto, and the more recent achievements of Safdie and Johansen. They also refer to the past, to Borromini, Michelangelo, Rossetti, Brunelleschi, to the Middle Ages, late antiquity, Hadrian's Villa, Greek acropolises, and even to prehistory—to show that the modern language of architecture is not merely the language of modern architecture; it enfolds the heresies and dissonances of history, those countless "exceptions to the rule" which have finally been emancipated and which can provide the backbone of an alternative language.

Participation is the rallying cry of young people, politicians, sociologists, and artists. There is a considerable element of demagogy in that cry. What does taking part mean in architecture? Giving the man in the street a T-square and compasses and telling him to design anything he likes? He would only ape the most backward classical models. It does not mean offering him several plans and asking him to take his pick. What criteria would he follow? Interpreted this way, participation is nothing more than a slogan. Instead, it is a substantial corollary of the seven invariables of the modern code.

Every one of the invariables, from listing functions to reintegration, demands participation, for they are concerned with the formative process (not with form), with the unfinished, with an architecture that can grow and change, an architecture that is not isolated but can communicate with external reality and even soil its hands with kitsch. Nobody wants "beautiful" consolatory objects any more. Art has stepped down from its pedestal to meet life halfway and assimilate the esthetic valences of the ugly and the cast-off. Alberto Burri paints rags; Claes Oldenburg discovers the message in a "soft typewriter"; noise is not antimusic but rather "alternative music"; and in architecture, the Mummers Theater looks as if it had been built with junk bought from a scrap dealer.

The unfinished in art has a long history, from Mnesicles to Rossetti and Palladio, reaching its high point in Michelangelo. Contemporary art, however, codifies the unfinished by the completion of an interrupted communicative process, requiring action by the user. Thus participation is not a paternalistic sop but an inherent feature of the coming-into-being of an open work of art. Take city planning. Classicists envisage total city plans that can be carried out only in dictatorial regimes. Modern architects, instead, fight for open and continuous planning that can answer

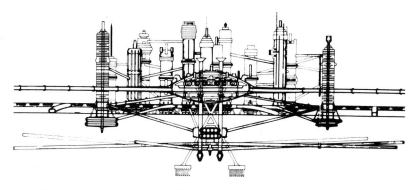

25. "Design for a city design": Plug-in City, by the British Archigram group. Dense urban concentration, forests of skyscrapers connected at various levels and functionally reintegrated, extensive green areas all around. This sort of organization would also contribute to a more intense community life.

society's new demands at any moment. The classicists design Renaissance "ideal cities" that are abstract, utopian, and perpetually frustrating. The moderns know that they cannot design a real city, they can only design its tentative design; that is to say, they can develop a hypothetical program for the future, but one that will be carried out with different and unexpected forms as needs change.

The unfinished approach is the goal of the seven invariables, and it is a fundamental prerequisite if architecture is to be involved in the land- and townscape, assimilate its contradictions, and rummage in squalor and kitsch in search of human values that need saving. Sociologists have found that slums, *bidonvilles, favelas,* and *barriadas* have an intensely vital sense of community that is unknown in "planned" lower-class housing developments. Why is that? Because adventure, the pioneering spirit, and neighborliness are missing in planned settlements, together with that spontaneous kitsch which, despite its negative features, can be extremely stimulating. In the modern language of the unfinished, participation is the indispensable structural complement of architecture in action.

There it is. The seven invariables provide a guide to design. No architect, certainly not Wright, Le Corbusier, Mies, or Aalto, would subscribe to them in toto, although Johansen and Safdie might. They are seven heresies, seven testimonies against classical idolatry, intolerable if taken all at once. Small matter. With this guide in the pocket, each will apply them as far as he can. Some will not apply them at all. Herbert Marcuse (*An Essay on Liberation,* 1969) calls people like that "the mad ones, the uncommitted, those who take flight into all kinds of mysticism, the fools and the scoundrels, and those who couldn't care less whatever happens."

Afterthoughts

1. COMING OF AGE

Throughout architectural history, linguistic codification has marked a culture's coming of age. What is it that conventionally distinguishes history from prehistory? The discovery of writing, that is, an institutionalized way of communicating. Of course, even before writing there were instruments of transmission, but at a restricted level. Likewise architects, for better or for worse, have communicated ideas and experience even without a formalized idiom at their disposal. But only now can one speak, read, and write architecture outside a restricted specialist milieu. This achievement transcends the framework of the discipline and implies democratic development, a new social era for architecture based on a consensus that is not paternalistic, populist, or pretentious (where real needs are constantly mixed up with those created by advertising), but authentic and direct.

Many architects are afraid to grow up. They prefer to remain dependent children under the authority of a father figure. But in the 1950s and 1960s the fathers—Wright, Le Corbusier, Gropius, Mies van der Rohe, Mendelsohn, and, a few years later, Louis Kahn—died. Moreover, some of them stopped nourishing their children long before they actually died: Mies, for example, when he began working with closed prisms and abandoned the poetics of fluid spaces channeled by De Stijl free plans; and Gropius, when he turned to teamwork in America and forgot the system of breaking blocks up into functional volumes, which had been the great achievement of the Bauhaus. Even Le Corbusier, when he took his giant step forward at Ronchamp, left teaching behind and disinherited children and grandchildren, who had to fall back on the Le Corbusier "manner" of the Lyons La Tourette monastery and Chandigarh.

There are no more father figures. It is time to grow up, get free of "adult" guardianship, and speak an independent codified language that derives naturally from the work of the masters but is not dominated by their individual styles and the weight of their overwhelming personalities.

Is there any other alternative? None that does not carry infantilism to grotesque extremes. Some orphan architects, without a father to turn to, head back to the maternal womb of the academy, the classicist ideology of power, geometric dogmas, harmony, and proportion. In short, in their anxiety for security, they commit suicide. Others fall into the opposite error. Rather than accept the modern language, they push back "zero degree" to the limit of chaos and anticulture and reject any system of communication.

The stages of development in music are clear: atonality, Expressionist destructuring; then, dodecaphonic rationalism; and, finally, postdodecaphonic aserial music, which eschews rationalist rigor, but not in the name of despair and chaos. These stages are less evident in architecture, because Expressionist zeroing (Gaudí and later Mendelsohn) did not precede rationalism but evolved almost contemporaneously with it from the beginning of the century to the early twenties. Thus the postrationalist organic era is full of Expressionist revivals, especially in the serpentine forms of Aalto. Even the Ronchamp chapel is a mixture of Expressionism and *Art Informel* with occasional elements of "Baroque persuasion" in the lighting, sometimes seductive and sometimes overstated. It is worth stressing the point that there are two refuges in the maternal womb: academic classicism and pseudo-Baroque Expressionism. The latter may seem more complex and hypnotic, but it is no less naïve and regressive than the former.

2. MANNERISM AND LANGUAGE

Is it really indispensable that there be a codified language? If its invariables are derived from architectural masterpieces, is it not enough to follow those precedents? In other words, why pass through a code, which is necessarily reductive, instead of going straight to the original sources?

Certainly, before the constants of the modern language of architecture were formulated, the only historically legitimate path was Mannerism. At a theoretical level, there is nothing wrong with that. On the contrary. Mannerism humanizes the styles of geniuses by divesting them of the messianic attitude of a Wright or the doctrinarianism of a Le Corbusier. If Mannerism could make these styles truly popular and available to all, there would, of course, be no need to codify an architectural language. Unfortunately this is not the case. Mannerism neither popularizes nor democratizes. It is a highly intellectual operation and almost untransmittable. Take, for example, Rosso Fiorentino and Pontormo, the occasional followers of Michelangelo and Borromini, the disciples of Wright, Le Corbusier, and Mendelsohn; they amount to a few dozen in the whole world. Why is this the case? Because Mannerists work from results, from finished products, and neglect the process that developed the products. What they do might be called "speech about speech." Mannerists elaborate on forms, not on structure and formation. They annotate and distort forms in a sagacious but limited and aristocratic way. The works of the masters are derived from the reality of life. The works of the Mannerists are derived simply from those of the masters. The masters continually destructure, they go back to the starting point, and they return to listing functions directly. The Mannerists, on the other hand, perceive reality only through the filter of selected and exalted images. Thus Mannerists tire quickly and are sucked back into the academy, which is always lying in ambush (neo-sixteenth-centuryism, neoclassicism, contemporary neohistorical trends).

It is important to bear in mind the genetic weakness of Mannerism: the only way it can destroy classical models—either tear them apart in anger or undo them with irony—is by preserving those models as emblems of a sanctity to be desanctified. To challenge their authority the Mannerists must first acknowledge it. The infractions and dissonant notes of the Mannerists presuppose the tyranny of classical harmony. Indeed Mannerism has nothing to work on when it encounters anticlassical methodologies, as in the buildings of Michelangelo, Borromini, or Wright. Without the despotic reign of the academy, the Mannerists have nothing to struggle against, and their invective is hushed to a murmur.

A direct unmediated passage from the writing of the masters to the common language of the people does not and cannot exist. It would be absurd to tell people to go back to the sources, to read the *Divine Comedy* in order to learn Italian. If a language is to be spoken by everybody, some invariables must be distilled from the works of poets so that it becomes possible to communicate in everyday prose.

3. THE HISTORIC SEQUENCE OF THE INVARIABLES

Can the sequence of the seven invariables be modified at will? For example, can reintegration come before antiperspective three-dimensionality, or space in time precede listing functions?

This sort of question ignores the historical genesis and gradual development of language. The invariables are not axioms outside of time, absolute truths, but stages marked by specific experiences. William Morris destructured the classical code, took it back to zero degree; and he championed listing, the inventorying of functions, and freedom from canons of symmetry, proportion, orders, axes, alignments, and relations of full and empty spaces. Dissonance marks a later stage. It is not sufficient merely to register functional requirements; one becomes truly aware of them by noting their contrasts. Clearly, then, the first two invariables cannot be interchanged. Antiperspective three-dimensionality developed alongside Expressionism and especially with Cubism, when the object was no longer observed from a privileged viewing point but dynamically, from innumerable points of view. The result was four-dimensional decomposition, the analytical syntax of the De Stijl group. How could De Stijl precede Cubism, when it is one of Cubism's applications? Perhaps the fifth invariable, that is, the involvement of every architectural element in the structural play, could be moved, since it derives from all of modern engineering. But Wright, in the last of his eight sketches reproduced above, correlates it with the poetics of projecting structures and with the dismembering of the box into dissonant panels. As for infusing space with time, this occupies the sixth place, and it could not be otherwise. In effect, this invariable applies the volumetric techniques of Cubism to the cavities, the vital hollow spaces, the special places of architecture. Finally, it is superfluous to repeat that one cannot reintegrate what has not been separated. Otherwise it would be a question of a priori integration and a retreat to classicism.

The sequence of the seven invariables has been established by a historical process that lasted more than a century, and it cannot be altered without serious consequences. Every architect must follow the single stages of this itinerary, always referring back to the preceding invariables, without omission, that is to functional listing, the annihilation of every convention and set phrase, and the radical destructuring of the traditional architectural apparatus.

The modern language is a precise and almost ruthless instrument of criticism, a kind of litmus paper that scientifically determines whether and to what degree an architect is modern. Take Alvar Aalto, for example. His work incorporates listing, dissonance, antiperspective three-dimensionality, cantilevers, space in time, and reintegration, six invariables magnificently applied. What is missing, however, is four-dimensional decomposition, so that the reintegration in Aalto's works is uncertain, based as it is on the revival of Expressionist and even Baroque themes.

It is not compulsory to apply all the invariables, but their sequence must be respected. Gropius' work has listing, dissonance, antiperspective three-dimensionality, and volumetric decomposition; it ignores space in time and reintegration. Mies's European works are a triumph of decomposition and the spatial dynamics that derives from it. But in America he neglected first functional listing and dissonance and then antiperspective three-dimensionality; hence he reverted to academicism. What about Le Corbusier? He explored all the invariables, but not simultaneously. In his rationalistic buildings, listing and reintegration are missing, although the latter is splendidly present in the town plan for Algiers. He rarely decomposed, and when he did it was in the inhibited purist sense. At Ronchamp he inventoried and reintegrated, he stressed antiperspective three-dimensionality and introduced time into space. He broke things down, but he did not decompose them.

The seven invariables can be found all together in some of Wright's buildings and to a maximum degree in Falling Water, the *Divine Comedy* of the modern language of architecture.

4. MISUNDERSTANDINGS OF THE "LANGUE/PAROLE" RELATIONSHIP

It often happens that semiotic research uses new instruments to old ends and unconsciously fosters recrudescences of the academy.

One mistake is to exclude masterpieces and exceptional works, the products of creative geniuses, when codifying a language, and to take into consideration only "typical" or "paradigmatic" buildings, which represent the average standard. This is to neglect the fact that, lacking a code to make it generally accessible, the modern language has been unable to influence much of contemporary construction, which communicates only questionable and not very meaningful thoughts. Excluding masterpieces castrates the modern language. What remains is mediocrity, and that is always academic. The opposite procedure should be followed. Rules should be derived from exceptions, this is the only way the new language can become flesh.

The Italian language, for instance, was formalized on the basis of the most important texts, from the *Divine Comedy* on. Once structured, the language was assimilated at all levels, even that of everyday speech. The same thing can happen in architecture. The invariables derived from masterpieces can be applied correctly by even the humblest builders. But it is vain to seek for the invariables in "typical" or "paradigmatic" works, which are such precisely because they do not incorporate the invariables.

People spoke Italian long before a codification was derived from the *Divine Comedy*. The same sort of thing is true in architecture. There are peasant houses, small factories, and vernacular structures, "architecture without architects" in short, which have spontaneously applied the seven invariables. The language of the *Divine Comedy* arose from the vernacular. That poem legitimized an impulse from below and, once codified, resulted in the Italian language. Likewise Falling Water, the product of protracted travail against academic scaffoldings, provides the basis for a popular architectural language.

Some semiologists insist that architecture is made of rules and exceptions, but that only the rules can be codified. What rules? Since modern architecture is composed exclusively of exceptions, the only rules there can be are those of the academy. If we codify those rules, we run the risk of regressing to the Beaux-Arts preconception of harmony as the rule and dissonance as the exception. This is the opposite of what modern music showed to be the case when it established dissonance as the rule. Theodor Adorno makes this clear: "The most advanced technical procedures in music set problems that expose the resources of traditional [read: classical] harmony as a set of useless clichés. There are modern compositions in which occasional tonic harmonies appear, but it is this harmony, and not dissonance, which is cacophonous . . ." (Max Horkheimer and Theodor W. Adorno, *Dialektik der Aufklärung,* 1947). In architectural terms: academic rules, not the modern invariables, are arbitrary and incongruous. Adorno goes on to say that "the predomination of dissonance seems to destroy the rational 'logical' relationships in tonality [read: symmetry, proportion, geometric schemes, equilibrium of full and empty, balance of masses, axiality, perspective alignment, and so forth], that is, the simple relations of perfect harmony. In this, however, dissonance is more rational than harmony, for it offers to view, in an articulate although complex manner, the relationship of the sounds that go into it, instead of creating a unified 'homogeneous' mix that suppresses the individual components. . . ." Applying this principle to architecture, conventional set phrases without semantic value are always harmonic, tonal, and classicist, while meaningful messages are dissonant and express the reality of things and behaviors. It would be a serious mistake to think, as Mannerists do, that dissonance is possible only in contrast to harmony, which reduces dissonance to a mere exception to the rule of tonality. This is not the case. To quote Adorno again, "the new harmonies are not innocent successors to the old consonance; rather, they are distinct in that their unity is totally self-articulated. The single sounds unite to form a harmony, but within that harmony they can be distinguished one from another as single sounds. In this way they continue to be 'dissonant,'—not in respect of some sort of unachieved harmony but in themselves."

How many years, how many decades will it take to convince architects of what music has long since mastered? Freedom frightens them, and they demand harmonic consistency at all costs. Since life is packed with dissonance, they prefer to take it in at second hand by way of an a priori order. They practice self-censorship and impoverish the language of architecture. They really ought to hang the following quotation from Adorno on their studio walls: "The cult of consistency leads to idolatry. Material is no longer shaped and articulated to serve an artistic purpose. Instead the preordained arrangement becomes the artistic purpose. The palette takes the place of the picture." In architecture, the palette is all the fetishistic equipment of symmetry, proportion, perspective, and power-inspired monumentality.

Other semiologists say, we are interested not in the differences between classical and anticlassical idioms but in their similarities, the elements they have in common. This thesis only seems plausible, because classicism is not a language, but rather a linguistic ideology with no real basis, not even in the architectural works of the Greco-Roman world or the Renaissance. This is the crux of the matter: to deny the existence of a gap between architectural theories and real buildings, between abstract Beaux-Arts interpretations and the concrete languages of Greek, Roman, and Renaissance architecture is tantamount to enlisting semiotics in the cause of reaction. There is no point in searching for a meeting ground between the classical and the anticlassical, for all valid architects, ancient and modern alike, have been anticlassical. Since classicism is an artificial power-inspired construct, it is perhaps comparable to the formal Latin that was exhumed in the fifteenth century for the use of an elite that wanted to avoid the problems of a living language. Would it not be absurd to look for what fifteenth-century Italian and courtly Latin have in common?

Ferdinand de Saussure's dichotomy of *langue* and *parole* has generated innumerable misunderstandings in architectural theories, for two reasons: first, *langue* has been interpreted not as the concrete language of buildings but as the contrary, formal Beaux-Arts ideology; second, as a consequence, the *paroles,* i.e., the creative acts, have been interpreted as exceptions and anomalies, not to be assimilated by the *langue* but to be excluded from it.

In verbal language, *paroles* start out as exceptions and then filter into the normal *langue*. In architecture, instead, they always remain exceptions, because the *langue* of classicism is not a real language, but an abstract ideology refractory to anything new. What *paroles* of Michelangelo or Borromini have ever found their way into the classical language? Not one, as might be expected from a pseudo-language that is frozen by its very nature. The same thing can be said of Wright, Le Corbusier, Gropius, Mies, Mendelsohn, and Aalto, whose "words" left the Beaux-Arts system untouched.

The difficulties that arise in discussions with Saussure's followers derive from their assumption that the true language of architecture is classical. We know that it is anticlassical and always has been. For us, then, the language of architecture is composed exclusively of *paroles* and is dissonant, while for them, *paroles* cannot exist without a *langue,* and hence the architectural *paroles* must be referred to the non-*langue* of classicism, with disastrous results.

5. THE SEVEN INVARIABLES IN TOWN PLANNING

Town planning is so closely related to architecture that one can legitimately speak of "urbatecture." The seven invariables are equally applicable to buildings, cities, and whole regions. Is not inventorying functions the first thing to do in preparing a city plan? Is not dissonance indispensable to keep zoning from being monotonous? Likewise, antiperspective three-dimensionality provides the means to counter the mania for monumental axes, chessboard street systems, and predetermined geometrical spaces, be they square, rectangular, round, or hexagonal. Breaking up the building box is like breaking up the closed plan of the classical city. And space in time? This is just as applicable on the urban scale as it is on the architectural level. And reintegration seems ever more urgent and fruitful in city planning if life is to be infused into organisms that have been zoned to death.

Urbatecture. To reintegrate the city means to reweave its very fabric and give new drive to the various functions of its coefficients. It has been remarked more than once that schools are low-use structures if the city segregates them in separate areas. A school is unused for several hours of the day, all night, on holidays, and during long vacations. This sort of waste is typical of almost all public buildings (theaters, movie houses, government offices, churches, and so forth) and can be eliminated only by reintegrating educational, social, administrative, productive, commercial, and recreational functions in a new organization that is different from the present city. In town planning as in architecture, the modern language abhors economic and cultural waste.

One beneficial result of the anticlassical code should be the overcoming of a frustration that has plagued city planning at least since the middle of the fifteenth century, when "ideal cities" were conceived according to geometric patterns, with their grill or radial schemata. These oppressive, despotic, and totalitarian layouts are fostered by authority to contain social life within an ironclad implacable "order." Fortunately these ideal cities were never built, despite some negligible attempts. But for centuries the "ideal city" has been doing serious damage to town planners' psyches. Their megalomaniacally rigid programs have never made headway, and planners have developed neurotic persecution complexes. They feel unappreciated because urban development remains oblivious to their work. Politicians, administrators, businessmen, rich and poor alike display the greatest indifference to their plans. With a few exceptions, city planners have never understood the reason for their lack of success. With no sensitivity to social dynamics, but endowed with a driving mania for grandeur, they have always tried to regiment society in static, inhuman, and suffocating constructs. The proof is that "ideal cities" have been built chiefly for four emblematic functions: military bases, insane asylums, prisons, and cemeteries. Rectangular, circular, hexagonal, and radial plans have found full expression in military installations from the Roman camp on, and in jails. They are fine for places where men are rigidly disciplined or imprisoned, from the Regina Coeli jail in Rome to Leavenworth. This sort of city is "ideal" only for the powers that be. Even in the field of military architecture, however, there have been rebellious spirits who rejected the code of geometry. Suffice it to mention Francesco di Giorgio, Sanmicheli, and Michelangelo's 1529 plans for the Florence fortifications.

What is particularly symptomatic is the fact that the great heretics of architectural history—Brunelleschi, Michelangelo, Palladio,

26–28. Three plates with Michelangelo's sketches for the Florence fortifications of 1529. *Preceding plate:* interior spaces. *Above:* structural profiles. *Following plate:* some shapes of the ramparts toward the outside; walls-landscape dialogue.

and Borromini—never drew up a city plan. They put their stamp on whole cities, true, but without a priori constraints. Theirs was a ferocious and passionate dialogue with the urban organism. These men took it apart and possessed it, they calculated its development by focal points and nodes of activity, careful never to block its flexibility. It is no paradox to say that the only people not needed in city planning are city planners. Is it conceivable that a city planner rather than an urbatect like Biagio Rossetti could ever have built the Ferrara of the Estes?

Does the modern language of architecture repudiate city planning? Certainly not. It repudiates classical planning, which is not based on inventorying functions, dissonance, antiperspective vision, dismembering of the box, space in time, and organic coordination. How, then, can we draw up plans and direct the development of cities and regions? We may follow the lead of contemporary painting, which rejects the "finished" object and requires that the observer mentally complete the picture himself. Like architecture and even more than architecture, city planning must arise from an interplay of open hypotheses that can be accepted, modified, or reoriented by society according to its own complex and varied needs. It is a question of taking part in city life from within—not passively but energetically day by day and without the rigid authoritarian a priori principles of geometric "order."

6. QUESTIONS AND ANSWERS ABOUT ARCHITECTURAL WRITING

Is there not a risk that the codification of the modern language of architecture will lead to a new academicism? Will not the seven invariables tend to become precepts like those of the Beaux-Arts school, albeit in the opposite direction?

This question is typical of many architects' mentality. Imaginary specters are invented to avoid the responsibility of trying out something new. Why not try, instead, to design a building or teach a course in design based on these invariables? The doubts will vanish the minute you start listing functions.

Language concerns forms of communication, but is not the present problem rather concerned with the content of those forms? And, in the last analysis, does not the architect's role in society depend on that very content?

The first invariable, inventorying, is specifically concerned with functional content, building programs, and social behavior. If this invariable is neglected, the whole construct falls apart or, rather, makes no sense because there is nothing to express in dissonance, nothing to decompose and reintegrate. This proves that the modern language will not tolerate alibis or excuses. If the question of content is evaded, there can be only regression to classicism.

A system of criticism based on the invariables may provide criteria for judging a finished building, but what about a design, and especially a city plan?

The invariables provide a precision instrument for checking every stage of design, from the preliminary sketch to the final working drawings. This has been verified a hundred times at the drawing board and in the classroom. Of course in a rough plan you cannot, for example, estimate the exact degree of dissonance or four-dimensional decomposition. But the critical method is still appropriate; one asks, can the design at this stage still accommodate the principle of dissonance and decomposition? If the answer is no, then the design is closed, reactionary, and classicist and should be repudiated. In the first stages, functional listing alone may be enough. But one must make sure that the design is sufficiently open to accommodate the other invariables.

The act of designing is not carried out in stages, applying one invariable after another. Usually architects work in synthetic fashion conceiving the whole design at once. So how can the seven invariables be applied?

They must be used to make sure that the synthesis, which is perfectly legitimate in itself, is not rigid. One does not have to start with analysis before proceeding to synthesis, but if the synthesis cannot pass the functional and semantic test, it means that it has fallen into classicism.

Is it ever possible to reach total zero degree culturally? Does Barthes' "zero degree in writing" really exist? Do not creative spirits make revolutions by taking what is positive from the past and the present and incorporating it into their vision of the future?

Suffice it to consider the relationship between Latin and Italian. The vulgar tongue brought Latin to zero degree in the sense that it destructured its code. True, it retained several elements, but it took them out of the context of the old language and gave them a different context. In the same way, modern architecture takes what is good from the past and reveals its anticlassical essence. It rejects and annihilates not the past but the corruption of it that was carried out by Beaux-Arts norms.

But why condemn symmetry, which is so common in ancient architecture and even raises its head in several works by Wright?

Cesare Beccaria, writing about crime and punishment (*Dei delitti e delle pene,* 1764), was interested in prisons, not in free democratic communities. Yet he said, "It is a false sense of utility that would try to give a multitude of people that symmetry and order which only inanimate material can absorb." That epigraph ought to be carved on the drawing boards of architects and city planners. If a building is conceived as an inanimate monumental object, only to be looked at and not to be used, then symmetry is fine, because it is a perfect reflection of political and bureaucratic authoritarianism. But if a building must perform specific functions and accommodate particular contents, it cannot be symmetrical, because symmetry, like harmony in music, binds every element to what has gone before and what comes after and to what is above and below. Symmetry sacrifices the particular and individual on the altar of overall design, which is uniform, hierarchical, and unalterable. As for Wright, it must be said that you cannot invent a new language in a single day. He had to fight the reigning classicism (architectural "Latin"), and there is nothing scandalous in the fact that he sometimes used partially symmetrical schemes. But what is more important in Wright, the rare leftovers of tradition or his revolutionary messages? The academic eye concentrates on whatever is obsolete in a genius, from Brunelleschi to Palladio. What we should look at are their original achievements. Why is there such fear of dissonance and asymmetry? The linguist Giacomo Devoto wrote in *Il linguaggio d'Italia:* "It is strange that qualified scholars are so reluctant to accept the fertile principle of the contraposition of the marginal and the central, which has marked the great transition from one-dimensional to two-dimensional linguistics, in preparation for the three-dimensional discipline of modern sociological linguistics." Symmetry flattens and diminishes, while our lexical needs are immense. As early as the first century B.C., Lucretius again and again deplored the *sermonis patrii egestas,* the poverty of the national idiom. And Devoto continues: "Plato's hypothesis of language as *nomos,* as 'law' or 'convention,' led to the concept of 'analogy.' What Plato called language's 'creativity' or *energeia* led to the doctrine of 'anomaly.' . . ." Devoto's incisive verdict on the Italian language could also be applied to architecture: "A selective, classicist, subjective exigency, and hence an impoverishing one, won out over the functional exigency which enriches the idiom. This is a feature of the Italian language that has been felt throughout its history down to our own times." The fear of change leads to the geometric and to symmetry.

Nowadays no one is interested in problems of architectural language or in architecture generally. The challenge comes from outside the field and concerns the struggle for a new kind of city and a different environment. Why bother about the seven invariables?

To make the battle more successful and spirited. This came out clearly in regard to a housing project built in Rome in the Pietralata area. A group of leftist students set up a "protest display" about the conditions in that area. There were posters with photographs documenting the lack of service facilities, the demonstrations that had been staged by the residents, police action, and so on. They made a lot of noise, but there was very little in the way of concrete achievement in this protest. At a certain point, however, the students decided to make an analysis of the neighborhood in terms of the seven invariables. They produced more posters showing that none of the invariables had been applied in the design of the area. The display was no longer demagogic, and it was infinitely more persuasive.

Finally, why is it that the modern language of architecture has not been codified before? What caused this inexplicable delay, when the new language could have been used extensively in the profession and in the schools during these past decades of feverish building?

No answer to this anguished and almost obsessive question can provide anything more than mere consolation. One may cite a variety of reasons: (1) as long as the masters of the modern movement were still alive and active, the illusion persisted that some "manner" connected with their styles could take the place of a codified language; (2) structuralism, semiotics, and linguistics were not sufficiently developed to shake the world of architecture; (3) it took a total reduction to zero degree, not just in architecture but existentially as well, as in the Paris spring of 1968, to stimulate the codification of a democratic idiom. All these explanations are plausible, and others as well, but they are tautological. The question remains. Schoenberg created and codified the language of modern music. Wright, Le Corbusier, Gropius, and Mendelsohn created the language of modern architecture, but they did not codify it. Why? Why didn't someone else do it, then, and spare architecture decades of waste and destruction, false ideologies, and desperate flights into the past and future? In any case, the time has come to spread the democratic language of architecture.

29. The "Modulor" by Le Corbusier, a metric scale based upon golden sections and human measures (cartoon by Jan van Goethem). Corbu's purism simplifies the process of Cubism in a classical key. Conscious of this danger, Le Corbusier denied the purist trend from the Chapelle de Ronchamp on.

PART TWO: *Architecture versus Architectural History*

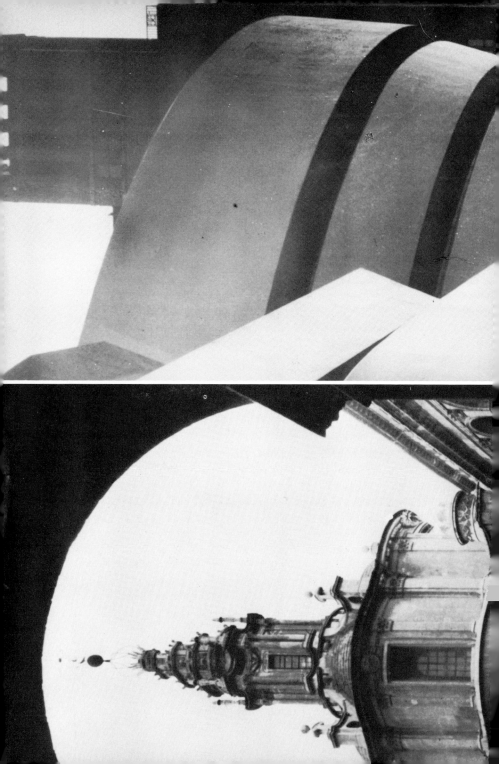

Preceding pages:
30–31. A meeting ground of two architectural geniuses: Borromini's spiral atop Sant'Ivo alla Sapienza, Rome (1642–60), and Wright's helicoidal Guggenheim Museum, New York (1946–59).
Above:
32–37. Historiography passively registered in nineteenth-century revivals: neo-Greek (British Museum, London), neo-Roman (Panthéon, Paris), neo-Medievalism (Prison, Würzburg), neo-Gothic (Trinity Church, New York), neo-Renaissance (Haughwout Building, New York), and neo-Baroque (Opéra, Paris).

Introduction: Anticlassicism and Le Corbusier

In Part One I showed that the present-day architectural code concerns not only the masters of the nineteenth and twentieth centuries but all architects who, over the span of history, fought against dogma, hallowed and entrenched precepts, a priori ideologies and theories of style, formal taboos, and the canons of classicism.

The modern language emerged and matured out of a simultaneously creative and critical commitment which, on the one hand, stands for the right to speak architecture in a way that differs from the classical and, on the other, explores history in the search for new roots in the past. We "write" architecture in a different language because we "read" it in a heterodox frame of mind. The impulse to write coincides with that of rereading the ancient texts and thus avoiding false interpretations. Architects have thrown off the strictures of classicism. Similarly, historians spurn academic methods of examining and judging monuments. In fact, the critic, from Baudelaire to van Doesburg, is oftentimes one with the artist.

How has the time-space language, from nineteenth-century eclecticism to the present day, become structured? This is the theme of the present study, which will trace the dialogue between architecture and historiography, and record the points of contact between linguistic invention and critical research. The breach between the old and the new architecture can be likened to the distance between, say, Latin and Italian or French, one an extinct tongue, the others living—with the difference, however, that classicism is not a real language but rather an ideology aiming to

91

codify any "style" by laying down abstract formulas and arbitrary regulations.

To begin with, we must repudiate two persistent misunderstandings. One is the romantic myth of the ascetic poet who stands aloof from all dialectic involvements with cultural and linguistic events. It is easy to prove that every authentic architect nurtures his inspiration by delving into the past. His elective affinities, however partial they may be, are more significant, generally, than those of the critics because he must face emergencies of the moment and resolve them. The second fallacy is that one can grasp modern architecture without a deep knowledge of its precedents. A brief survey of the cross purposes that marked the most important linguistic ruptures, from the present back to prehistory, will disprove this misapprehension once and for all.

As a point of departure, let us consider the most famous exponents of the modern movement, Frank Lloyd Wright and Le Corbusier. Both were endowed with strongly individualistic visions of architecture, yet they culled their ideas from definite historical contexts. Wright was a devotee of Henri Louis Sullivan, *"Lieber Meister,"* who, in turn, was dependent on the neo-Romanesque of Henry Hobson Richardson and, by opposition, on American eclecticism. Le Corbusier harked back to the origin of European rationalism, to the puritanism of Adolf Loos, enemy of the Vienna Secession, the Austrian counterpart of the Art Nouveau movement created by the Brussels architect Victor Horta in 1893 and spearheaded by Henry van de Velde, passionate apostle of the English Arts and Crafts school. With the Red House, built for William Morris in 1859, came the birth of modern architecture. But we can understand Morris' reform only if we put it within

---

38–44. A retrospective view of the modern architectural movement. *From the top:* Wright's Falling Water, Bear Run, Pennsylvania (1936–39) and Le Corbusier's Maison La Roche, Auteuil, near Paris (1923); Guaranty Building in Buffalo, by Dankmar Adler and Louis H. Sullivan (1894) and Adolf Loos's house in the Nothartgasse, Vienna (1913); Ames Gate Lodge in North Easton, Massachusetts, by Henry H. Richardson (1880) and railing of Victor Horta's studio, St. Gilles, Brussels (1898). *Below:* Red House, designed by Philip Webb for William Morris, Bexley Heath, Kent (1859), which marked the birth of the modern movement.

the context of the neo-Gothic culture anticipated as far back as 1747 in Horace Walpole's country mansion at Strawberry Hill, near London. The re-evaluation of the Middle Ages was a weapon wielded to combat neoclassicism, the origin of which can be traced back to the ambiguous position toward the Baroque of a Juvarra or a Vanvitelli. Now we can proceed faster. Mannerism, particularly Michelangelo's abrupt departures from the classical, linked the Baroque with the sixteenth century. The fifteenth-century reversion to the sixteenth was heralded by Bramante's arrival in Rome. Between the early Renaissance and the Gothic stands the cupola of the Duomo of Florence, work of Arnolfo di Cambio and Brunelleschi, as well as the humanistic examples in medieval language, such as San Miniato al Monte in Florence and the portico of the Civita Castellana cathedral. The continuity from Gothic back to Romanesque is well known. Thus, we arrive at Sant'Ambrogio in Milan, St. Martin in Tours, and the abbey in Cluny, begun around A.D. 960. The Romanesque world reverts to the High Middle Ages, to the church of San Pietro in Tuscania, to the caesuras which measure the nave of Santa Maria in Cosmedin in Rome, thence to the Byzantine cycle and the paleo-Christian tradition, which takes us to the first century A.D., to the Roman basilica of Porta Maggiore and the catacombs. The concept of "late ancient" refers to the close affinities between Christianity and Roman art, which sprang from a dual source: first, the Etruscan civilization, the Italic period, and European prehistory; and second, Hellenism and archaic Greece, which carried forward the Cretan culture and therefore the culture of the Near East, whose origins trail back, once more, into protohistory.

45–56. A backward glance from nineteenth-century eclecticism to prehistory. *From the top:* Horace Walpole's neo-Gothic country house at Strawberry Hill (1747) and Reggia at Caserta, by Luigi Vanvitelli (1752–74); Michelangelo's Palazzo dei Conservatori, Rome (1546), and Bramante's Tempietto di San Pietro in Montorio, Rome (1501); cupola of the Duomo in Florence, by Filippo Brunelleschi (1420) and church of San Pietro in Tuscania (eighth century); Catacombs of Domitilla, Rome (third century) and Roman aqueduct at Gard (Pont du Gard) near Nîmes (A.D. 14); the Parthenon at Athens (447–432 B.C.) and the palace at Phaestos (2000 B.C.); trade exchanges between Crete and the ancient Orient, and dolmen at Carnac, Britanny (about 1500 B.C.).

MICENE

CRETA

MESOPOTAMIA

EGITTO

To grasp the matrix of the language professed by Wright and Le Corbusier, we must go back to the fourth millennium B.C. and then travel in the aeons preceding the discovery of writing. What do we exclude? The Far East; Chinese, Indian, Japanese, and Russian architecture; African and pre-Columbian monuments of the Americas. Even this is inaccurate, not only because the Mexican pyramids of Cholula and Teotihuacán document the exchanges between the eastern Mediterranean and Central America, but mainly because Oriental and prehistoric influences supplied a parameter to modern art. References to Mayan culture and direct borrowings from the Japanese crop up frequently in Wright's work.

The analogies between the Middle Ages and the Arts and Crafts movement, Gothic and Art Nouveau, Renaissance and modern rationalism, Baroque and organic architecture—as well as the seven invariables of the contemporary language deriving from them—are the subject matter of the four chapters that follow, with a concluding section on prehistory. This leaves aside ancient Greece and Rome, a logical omission inasmuch as the new architecture has turned its back on the classicism formalized by the Beaux-Arts academy. But are the Hellenic and Roman arts truly irretrievable? Let us examine this question.

The Greek patrimony was first organized into a historical system in 1755 by Johann Joachim Winckelmann in his *Gedanken über die Nachahmung der Griechischen Werke in der Malerei und Bildhauerkunst,* and subsequently by James Stuart and Nicholas Revett in their *Antiquities of Athens* (1762), by the achievements of the Dilettanti Society (1769), and by Lord Elgin's sensational exploit in removing the Parthenon marbles to London in 1801. A mounting fervor for Hellenism was further stimulated by the Greek war of inde-

---

57–59. Monuments of extra-European cultures which have influenced the development of modern architecture. *Above:* Sun Pyramid at Teotihuacán, Mexico (second century), evidence of exchanges between Eastern Mediterranean culture and pre-Columbian America. *Center:* Temple of Quetzalcoatl at Teotihuacán, Mexico (ninth century), with decorations that inspired some of Frank Lloyd Wright's plastic experiments. *Below:* Phoenix Hall in the Temple of Byōdō-in, near Kyoto, dating back to the Heian period (1053). Besides Wright, ancient Japanese architecture influenced numerous European architects, including Bruno Taut.

pendence in 1821. The great archaeological digs of 1750–80 and the studies they sparked fomented the Greek Revival in Great Britain: the Bank of England (1795–1827), designed by John Soane, reinterprets the Corinthian order of the Temple of the Sybil at Tivoli; St. Pancras church (1819–22), by William Inwood, imitates the Erechtheum; while Robert Smirke consecrated the neo-Greek style in the British Museum (1823) in London. In Germany, Karl Gotthard Langhans conceived the Brandenburg Gate (1789) in Berlin in terms of the Propylaea of the Acropolis in Athens, and Leo von Klenze set about hellenizing the city of Munich from 1816, while Karl Schinkel, although a sometime devotee of the Gothic, adopted classic elements in the theater and in the "Neue Wache" in Berlin, as well as in the church of St. Nikolaus (1843–49) in Potsdam. The contagious fever for Greek models spread across the Atlantic and, from 1820 to 1860, infected the United States, where Benjamin Latrobe and William Strickland were the most ardent champions of the revival.

All this, however, is extraneous to our theme, since it makes no contribution to the development of the modern architectural language, in fact only hinders it. Such classicist structures as, for example, the Church of the Madeleine in Paris and St. George's Hall in Liverpool attest to the unconditional surrender of art to erudition: glacial, emphatic magnifications of museum plaster, which in northern Europe, however, virtually evaporated in the fog, and consequently had no real dependence on archaeological scholarship.

Heretical, on the other hand, in the anti-Beaux-Arts sense, was Le Corbusier's love for Greece. During a pilgrimage he made to

---

60–63. Le Corbusier's sketches of the Athenian Acropolis, published in *Vers une Architecture* (1923). *From the top:* the Parthenon seen from the Propylaea; a glimpse of the Propylaea from the stylobate of the Parthenon; the Acropolis, showing the "pure" volume of the Parthenon; the Temple of Athena.
Following pages:
64–69. *Left:* the Acropolis in Athens seen from the air; the crude rock at the foot of the Parthenon; the square lacunars of the Parthenon. *Right:* Le Corbusier's "pure" volume of the Villa Savoye at Poissy (1929); skyscrapers in Le Corbusier's cityscape of Antwerp (1933); a museum quad with unlimited expansion, designed by Le Corbusier (1939).

that country in his youth, he discovered architectural values completely obliterated by the revivalists. He indicated the anticlassic features of the Hellenic language as follows:

—the taste for isolated volumes, autonomous prisms in the light, freely situated over an irregular landscape and cast in elementary geometrical schemes, as exemplified by the squares of Phidias' lacunary ceiling—a prophecy of modern Purism;

—the urban grids of Priene, Miletus, and, in general, all the cities laid out according to Hippodamus' principles—grids similar to those of the contemporary metropolis;

—molding. On the suspended prism of Corbu's Villa Savoye at Poissy, we see sensuous, chromatic, curved planes as the culminating element of the "promenade architecturale." These *"objets à réaction poétique,"* infusing the rigid, rational stereometries with lyrical qualities, are the offshoots of the entases and echini, the fluting, and the thousand imperceptible inflections of a vibrant Greek arithmetic—plastic adjectives which become disruptive substantives in the Ronchamp block.

The knottiest problem confronting the modern architectural language was that of surmounting the Renaissance perspective vision. To solve it, Le Corbusier reverted to a classical language that predated perspective. He produced authentic testimonies from ancient Greece which clamorously confuted Beaux-Arts academic doctrines.

The influence of the Roman heritage on modern architecture is both hybrid and complex. It takes on the individual stamp of its mediators, from Palladio to neoclassic erudition. Not infrequently neo-Roman merged with neo-Greek. Robert Wood's tomes on Palmyra and Baalbek (1753–57) and the description of the palace of Diocletian in Split in *Architectural Antiquities of*

70–71. Le Corbusier and the Greek town grid. *Above:* plan of Priene, according to Patrice Bonnet. The Acropolis (end of the fourth century b.c.) is located near the top, close to the mountains. *Below:* plan of Chandigarh, capital of Punjab, India, layout by Le Corbusier. The Capitol with the main public buildings is located in the upper sector, close to the mountains.
Following pages:
72–73. Model of Chandigarh, with the grid system and the Capitol at the north.
Insert: Model of Priene, with the grid system and the Acropolis at the north.

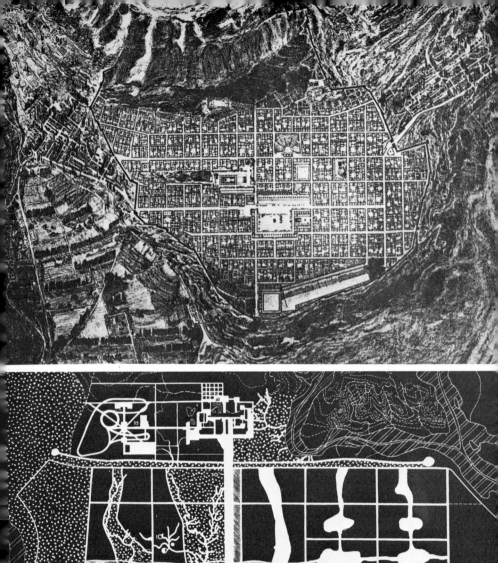
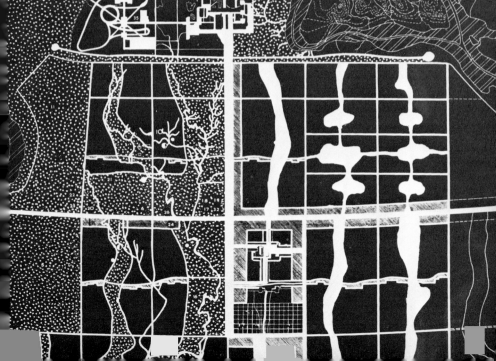

74–77. Separation of volumes from the ground, and plastic moldings in Greek culture and in Le Corbusier's work. *Left:* stylobate of the Temple of Afaia at Egina (fifth century B.C.) and a capital of one of the columns of the Propylaea at Athens (437–33 B.C.). *Right:* pilotis of Le Corbusier's Villa Savoye in Poissy (cf. 67) and interior of a house at Porte Molitor, Paris (1933).
Following pages:
78–80. Fluting and entasis of the Parthenon columns. Molded walls of Le Corbusier's Chapelle de Ronchamp (1950–53). The "objects with poetic reaction," discovered during the research carried out into Greek moldings, involve the structural organism (cf. 183).

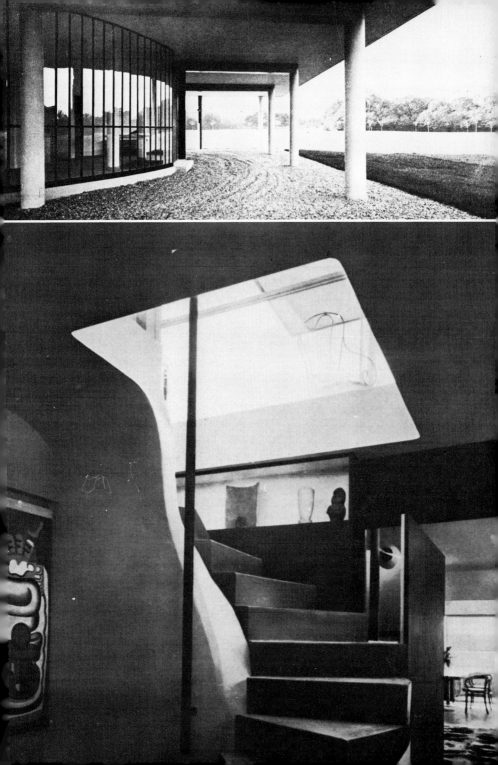

Rome (1821), by George Ledwell Taylor and Edward Cresy, stimulated elegant, flexible evocations, particularly in the United States where Thomas Jefferson created the uncommon beauties of Monticello (1790–1820) and recreated the Pantheon in the library of the University of Virginia without excessive philological compunction. Cold and pedantic, on the other hand, are numerous European buildings identified with the Roman revival. To cite a few: in Great Britain, St. George's Hall (1839), Liverpool, by Harvey Elmes and C. R. Cockerell, imitating the tepidarium of the Baths of Caracalla; in Paris, Germain Soufflot's Panthéon (1757–90) and Barthélemy Vignon's Madeleine (1806–42); in Italy, the works of Luigi Canina, Luigi Cagnola, and Pasquale Poccianti. The syncretic and adaptable nature of the ancient Roman constructions made imitations especially feasible where vast internal spaces were needed, such as bank interiors or the great hall of Pennsylvania Station (1906) in New York. But the Roman heritage leads to monumentalism, as witness even the stylized neo-Roman of Tony Garnier's stadium in Lyons and Paul Bonatz's railroad station in Stuttgart, not to mention the monstrous corruptions perpetrated in Italy by Marcello Piacentini, the Fascist architect.

No artist can be found who defied arrogant academic exegesis to point out the orignal qualities of Roman architecture in modern terms. Instead, this challenge was met in 1895 by the historian Franz Wickhoff in his book *Die Wiener Genesis* and, in 1901, by Alois Riegl in *Spätrömische Kunstindustrie*. Both authors identified Rome's special contribution in the "method of continuing narration," in the filmlike procession of figures spiraling on the Trajan and Antonine columns; in the stage sets wholly built for the amphitheaters which, unlike the Greek theaters, were never situated in positions where they could use the landscape as backdrops;

---

81. Cross vaults in Hadrian's Villa, Tivoli (A.D. 118–38). Ancient Roman architecture prompted one of the nineteenth-century revivals, exemplified by the Panthéon in Paris, by Germain Soufflot (cf. 33). Only very few artists could be inspired by ancient Rome without regressing into monumentalism, and this is why the "Romanist" trend was firmly rejected by modern architects. However, the "modernity" of the Roman language, particularly in the orchestration of interior spaces and in the "mode of continuing narration," was revealed by the Viennese historian Franz Wickhoff at the end of the last century.

and in the immense spaces of the basilicas and baths, with their soaring cupolas and vaults. Even when they conquered Greece, the Roman invaders crowded the acropolises, notably that of Olympia, with new gymnasiums, galleries, porticos, temples, and enclosing walls, blocking out the panoramic views. The "continuum," inherent in the very techniques of the conglomerate, saw its triumph during the reign of Hadrian and in the late Roman period, at Baalbek, at Split, and in the so-called Temple of Minerva Medica in Rome. It is not surprising that we find analogies between Hadrian's Villa at Tivoli and the Florida Southern College (1938) by Frank Lloyd Wright, or that an architect like Louis Kahn would take broad hints from Roman ruins to shape his ideas.

The development of modern architecture, therefore, progresses hand in hand with a cultural excavation, speaking figuratively, which drastically altered the methods adopted by traditional historiography and the results it had achieved. There is no gap between the way we write or speak architecture and the way we read it. If the misunderstanding that the contemporary code has broken away from the past persists and instigates reactionary attitudes grounded in pseudoenvironmental theories, this is only because too many among us are unable to cast off time-honored prejudices recognizing the modern, operational values of the ancient monuments and their pertinence to present-day problems. The purpose of this book is to show that the vitality of today's architectural language is one with the task of interpreting history in a modern, almost futuristic version, so as to make it act effectively as an incentive to creativity. The passive imitation that

---

82–84. Space in ancient Rome and its reflections in contemporary architecture. *Above:* Theater of Dionysus, Athens, a natural cavea with the city and surrounding landscape as its backdrop (330 B.C.). *Center:* Flavian Amphitheater (Colosseum), Rome, where all the visible scenery is man-built (A.D. 75–80). *Below:* Louis Kahn's project for the new Philadelphia (1956).
Following pages:
85–87. Convention Hall in Dacca, Bangladesh, by Louis Kahn (1970). The "Pecile" at Hadrian's Villa, Tivoli: sketch by Le Corbusier and view.

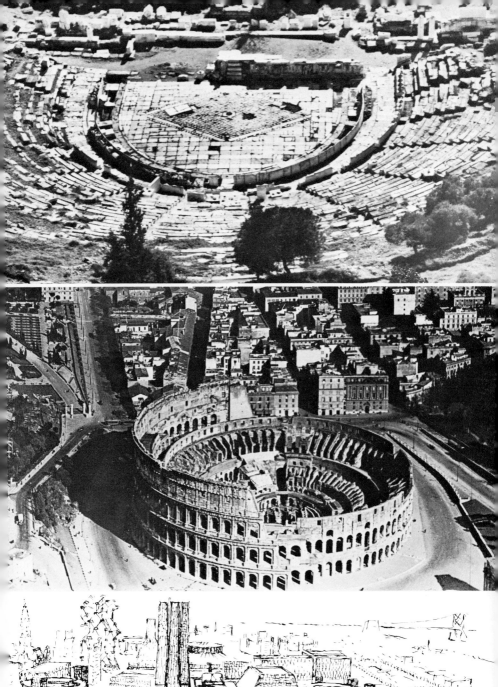

went with revivalism and the indifference of some avantguardists toward history are both deplorable and absurd. The historiographical revolution is an indispensable accomplice of the architectural revolution.

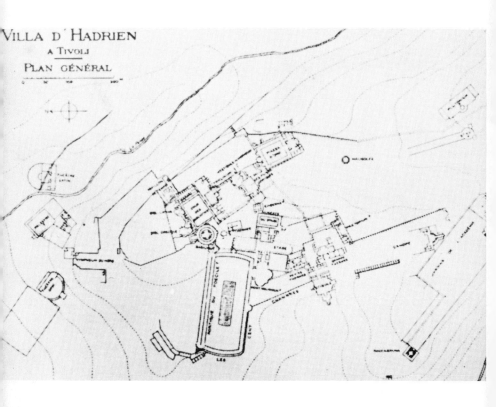

88–91. Hadrian's world and Frank Lloyd Wright. *Above:* general plan of Hadrian's Villa, Tivoli (cf. 92). *Right:* chapel, plan, and view of Florida Southern College at Lakeland, designed by Wright (1938–50).
Following pages:
92–93. Aerial view of Hadrian's Villa, Tivoli, with building sectors articulated by circular hinges and spread over the land. Aerial view of Florida Southern College, Lakeland, designed by Wright in a free, open schema that evokes the linguistic attributes of the age of Hadrian.

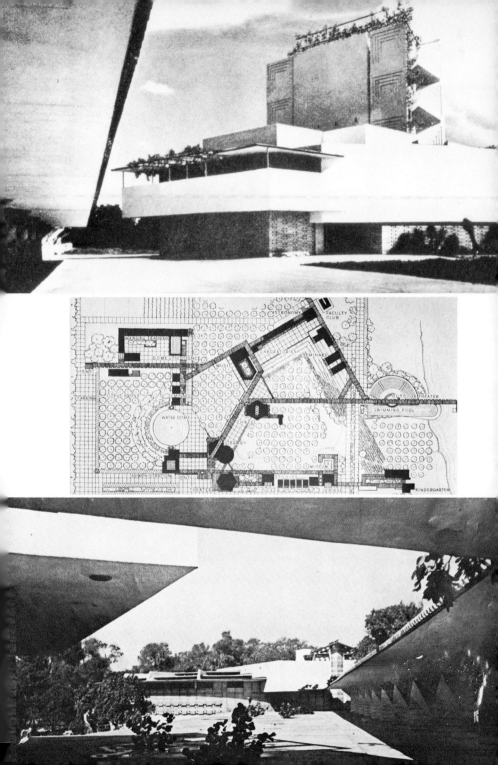

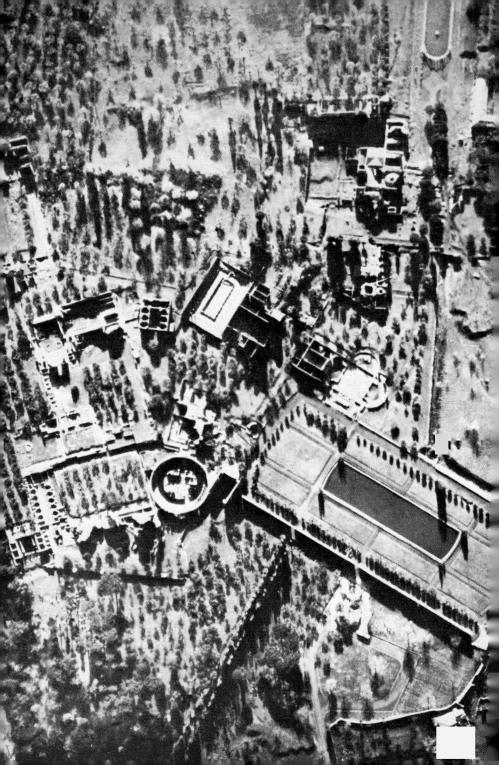

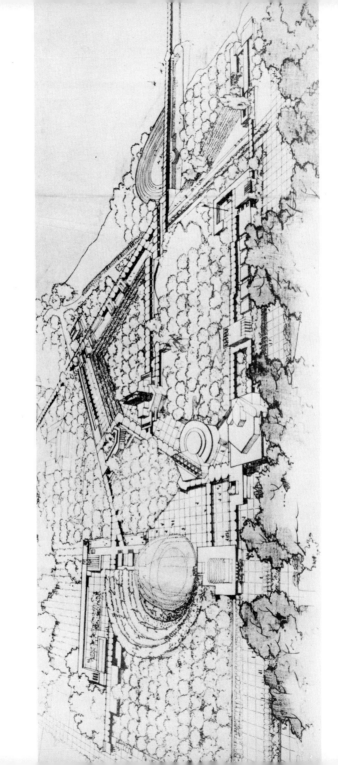

Preceding pages:
94. Medieval street in Perugia. Following the functional listing methodology, it is free of any a priori scheme.
Above:
95–96. Prison in Pittsburgh (1884) and Crane Library in Quincy, Massachusetts (1880), by Henry Hobson Richardson (cf. 42), master of American neo-Romanesque, which anticipated the same movement in Holland, led by Hendrik Petrus Berlage (cf. 104). With neoclassicism and neo-Gothic dominating the Beaux-Arts system, the Romanesque revival was instrumental in liberating architecture from the most dogmatic styles.

VIII

Medievalist Culture, Arts and Crafts, and Neo-Romanesque: Functional Listing as Design Methodology

John Ruskin (1819–1900) and William Morris (1834–96) headed the movement to re-evaluate the Middle Ages. British enthusiasm for the Gothic had been so enduring that it survived far beyond its own period and continued to thrive through the reigns of Elizabeth I, the Stuarts, and the four Georges despite the emphasis put on Renaissance architecture by Inigo Jones and Christopher Wren. Long before Ruskin published *The Seven Lamps of Architecture* (1849) and *Stones of Venice* (1851), Britons had been reading such widely diffused works as *Gothic Architecture Improved* (1742), by Batty Langley; *An Attempt to Discriminate the Gothic Styles* (1819), by Thomas Rickman; *The Architectural Antiquities of Great Britain* and *The Cathedral Antiquities of Great Britain* (1807–36), by John Britton. Of particular importance were the volumes of Augustus Pugin, *Specimens of Gothic Architecture* (1821) and *Examples of Gothic Architecture* (1831), as well as the more incisive and better known works by his son A. Welby Pugin, *Contrasts; or a Parallel between the Architecture of the 15th and 19th Centuries* (1836), *True Principles of Christian Architecture* (1841), and *An Apology for the Revival of Gothic Architecture in England* (1843), which brought the revolt against classicism to the boiling point.

In mid-century, therefore, Ruskin planted his ideas in a terrain already well seeded; it should be remembered that in 1836 the classicist Charles Barry, architect for Westminster Palace in London, had entrusted the Gothic-style ornamentations of this building to A. Welby Pugin. It was necessary, however, to give the medieval revival a different orientation, cutting it adrift from mystic moralism and secularizing it. To this end, the Romanesque precedents in Venice and all through northern Italy were of greater value than the impressive cathedrals of France and England. Both Ruskin and Morris focused on the social and ethical aspects of medieval expression and stressed its popular character more than its structural virtuosities. In fact, they belittled the nineteenth-century engineering feats of Brunel, Paxton, and Eiffel, spurred on in France by Eugène Viollet-le-Duc's theoretical contributions, as we shall see in the next chapter.

Everywhere medievalism proved to be the weapon for tearing down classicism. Even in a country like Italy, dominated by academic bias, Camillo Boito prefaced his book *Architettura del Medio Evo in Italia* (1880) with a trenchant essay, "On the Future Style of Italian Architecture," advancing theses already championed in England for over thirty years.

In this essay Boito aimed his deadly darts against the architects of the High Renaissance because they "froze even the charms and gaiety of country houses with colonnades, frontispieces, and the bombast of Roman public monuments. These agreeable retreats, where man seeks respite from life's fatigues (how well Horace discoursed on this subject!) should offer him all the combined pleasures of rest and tranquility; yet, with tiresome punctiliousness, those who designed them slavishly copied the exact proportions of Roman monuments, allowing for few spacious rooms, with windows that seemed to dread the surrounding nature and extremely high, dark, vaulted ceilings, thus turning delight into pompous boredom. Whoever wishes to measure the intelligence sixteenth-century architects applied to their imitations of Roman architecture should compare Pliny's villa with one of the most praised mansions conceived by a great craftsman amidst the blessed hills of Vicenza, the Rotonda of Capra. He will see that whereas the Romans invested their houses and villas with organic unity, in the Renaissance imitations the organism was captive, indeed it vanished under a preponderant, tyrannical symbolism. . . . This was an era of rules and precepts, when architecture was reduced to mere formulas, in a series of arithmetic relationships, in contrivances of a few pre-established forms. . . . This apish irrationality soon degenerated into ranting irrationality."

If this verdict on the sixteenth century and the Baroque sounds somewhat categorical, Boito's attack on neoclassicism smacked of sarcasm: "Architecture did not reach back to its sources, rather it was content with second-hand erudition, it imitated the imitators. Antonio Canova thought to build a vast and rich temple at his own expense, as indeed he did at Possagno, his birthplace. On the fifth of August 1818, he wrote to the architect Giannantonio Selva, 'I considered it wise to mention it only to a few of the best architects among us and tell them of my project and how I planned to execute it, that is, to follow the model of some famous monument, without adding any other invention to it.' Selva gave his approval just as the Roman architects and the San Luca Academy had already done. Soon after, Selva died, whereupon Canova sought the valued advice of Antonio Diedo, and explained that the atrium 'of the church is borrowed from the Parthenon and the other parts from other ancient temples.' We need not wonder that Canova was taken with such a passion for classicism that he would copy idolatrous temples in minute detail for a Christian church. Nor should it seem strange that others were of a like mind. But let us take note of Diedo's reply: 'In my opinion, the plan leaves nothing to be desired. The façade is superb, but may I boldly presume to express a doubt? That is, whether it is right to reproduce the Parthenon and all its defects without altering it in any minimal part, or whether to make some small modifications whereby to purge it of those defects. Such would be, I believe, to narrow the two end intercolumniations. Nor would I hesitate to make all the intercolumniations equal by putting the triglyph of the last column on the axis instead of on the angle.' This purifier of the Parthenon, whose ignorance was patently abysmal, was widely acclaimed in the Veneto region as architect and author of elegant prose. Describing the Church of the Redeemer in Venice, he cried, 'Here is the temple that eclipses all others, even the most exalted and marvelous.' But then a worry gnawed at his viscera because the height of the nave 'falls by about two feet from the harmonious mean,' and commented that this must have been an oversight of the builders since it was unthinkable that Palladio 'could have slept over a matter of such great moment.' Again, in a speech, Diedo lauded Selva for writing a 'dissertation on the Ionic volute, in which he developed the thoughts of the most renowned architects and plunged into the most abstruse researches with keen insight. Thus, architecture was being wasted on the homeopathic purges of the building it was aping, on the 'harmonious mean' and the 'abstruse researches' into the Ionic volute."

Boito was chiding the classicists twice over for their follies, first for designing buildings like so many boxes, axial, with head-on perspectives, dreary, antifunctional, and servile to the taboos of symmetry and proportion; and, second, for systematically betraying the very tenets of antiquity by which they professed to be inspired. They sacrificed both the past and the present to an ideological a priori and to Beaux-Arts design dogmatism. Boito called the situation in Italy, where academic conformity reigned, virtually critical: "We are a restless and lazy people. We take no trouble to study the ancients, and we battle against the new. We scorn originality and despise imitation. We are at once skeptical and ridden with prejudices, we are scholars yet we scoff at philosophy, we are well grounded in our judgments and yet naturally inconstant in our imagination. Classicism has burdened us with a patrimony of rhetoric, the neo-Catholic school with a patrimony of sentimentalism tinged with hypocrisy and malignance. These two literary influences, widespread but fortunately in decline, are ruining our schools and our arts."

Italian Eclecticism, in fact, never shared that irreverence which allowed other European and American architects to take the forms of various periods out of their historical context and blend them together in pastiches which, however horrible, at least demonstrated their free will. It was altogether puritan, it would never sanction any mixture of styles. Boito goes on: "Italian art critics counsel us to follow the Moorish style in our theaters, the Gothic in our churches, the Greek in our city gates, the Roman in our

---

97–99. *Above:* auditorium in the Palace of Catalonian Music, Barcelona (1905), by Lluís Domènech i Montaner, who championed an unorthodox Eclecticism taking past styles out of their context and mixing them together. *Center:* water tank in Leghorn (1809), by Pasquale Poccianti, exponent of "puritan" Eclecticism, who outlawed stylistic contaminations. *Below:* electric powerhouse at Trezzo d'Adda (1906), by Gaetano Moretti, the finest example of Italian neo-Romanesque, which appeared much later than Richardson's in the United States and Berlage's in the Netherlands.

stock exchanges, the medieval municipal in our civic buildings, English Tudor, Italian, or French Renaissance in our houses, and so on. A different architecture for every kind of structure. Some would like to see our cemeteries in Egyptian style, others would like us to borrow forms and concepts from the Chinese and Turks. A poet once sang—and with good reason: *'Toujours l'honnête homme ouvrit / La fenêtre des vieux âges / Pour aérer son esprit'* (The honest man always opens / The window of remote ages / To refresh his spirit). But we ventilate ourselves so much that a courtesan, as Shakespeare put it, would catch cold."

Hence, since a wholly new architecture "cannot spring from an architect's brain; cannot discard the past altogether; cannot blend a plurality of styles or ape any one of them; must be national; must stem freely from a single Italian style of bygone times but eliminate the archeological aspects of that style to be completely modern," what should be selected? "The architect must feel that he has in hand a style which adapts easily and responsively to every case; which offers some means of adorning every nonsymmetrical part of a structure when this is necessary; which is spared the tedious traits of preconceived forms; which is free of abstract rapports; which is as rich as need be, yet modest; which can employ tall, short, thick, or thin columns, high, low, wide, or narrow windows, mullioned or three-mullioned, cornices wide and jutting or merely suggested, big, sweeping archivolts or small, arched lintels, slim pilasters and stout buttresses, arches strong and soaring or small and slender, delicate ornamentation and massive foliage; which, in short, uses a language that abounds in words and phrases, unfettered in its syntax, imaginative and precise, poetic and scientific, fitting neatly into the expression of the most diverse and difficult ideas. We can find the essence of such a language in Lombard architecture and the municipal manners of the fourteenth century. . . . Indeed, in the Lombard style, which spread from the northern provinces to central Italy and the Naples area in the eleventh and twelfth centuries, decorum went together with economy. Constructions in cut stone, with small pieces and diagonal joints, had need of only small volumes; geometrical ornamentation and regular foliage were executed with intelligence but not too scrupulously; stone components and walls formed a single unit, ruling out keystones, hinges, and other such appendages which do so much damage to buildings. Finally, each part of the whole could stand out by itself, offering a chance to create singularly beautiful effects. Materials, labor, and installation were less costly and more useful than in any other type of architecture. Every ordinary element that could not be hidden without damage was designed with art: chimneys, roof gutters, water spouts, tiebeam bolts, conduits, dormers, and so on. The fourteenth-century municipal style possessed these virtues. To be sure, we must overlook such effusions as the mosaics of the Cosmati school, the inlays of the Florence Duomo, the spiral columns, the intricate perforations, the whims and caprices; but, even without them, what riches still remain to draw from the public palaces, the churches, the cloisters, and the houses of that great century! We boldly maintain that, over the coming years, the crude but fecund Italian style we call Lombard for want of a better term will become the architecture of the new Italy, however it may be developed, refined, and modernized."

A masterly diagnosis in disfavor of classicism, Boito's, but a weak therapy. Had his prediction come true, Italy would have leapt to the forefront of the modern movement. In any case, the fervent exhortation in behalf of the early Middle Ages sprang from the very same motives as those that impelled William Morris to champion the Arts and Crafts reform, which called for:

—an aptitude for description; a narrative, flexible design method. Modern building programs had become more and more diversified—houses, schools, factories, office blocks, railroad stations, hospitals, and so forth—but their specific function was masked behind pseudo-Greek and -Roman grandiosity, or behind the Renaissance orders, which imposed stern rules on axes, symmetry, proportion, and central perspective. Compared with the magniloquent classicist composition, any medieval street appears far more varied in its profiles, its outlines and unrepeated rhythms, appropriate to its functional requirements and dynamics of reality. In this independence from preconceived norms and stylistic formulas, we discover a pressing ethical commitment to preserve the close bond between architecture and daily life against the fatuities of revivalism.

—organic unity. If every element of a building can "stand out by itself," then it is rid of the dichotomy that typifies so much classic architecture: a box with rooms inside and a colonnade to dress up the box; or, as in Haussmann's Paris, first the façade and then the structure more or less adapted to it. The Lombard style rejected Byzantine mosaics as too precious and restored the value of materials and bare walls, thus capping a trend already evident in High Middle Ages constructions. Similarly, the Arts and Crafts movement was first marked in 1859 with the erection of William Morris' mansion dubbed "Red House" because it exposed brick—for decades hypocritically concealed under stucco—to show how the honest use of materials could offer "a chance to create singularly beautiful effects."

—free arrangement of volumes and spaces. Renouncing the tyranny of horizontal and vertical alignments and repetition in the placement of windows and doors, architecture projects the interior spaces in two or three dimensions, that is, on the building walls and volumes. The pioneers of the modern movement understood that the "picturesque" and "anecdotal" nature of the medieval language implied a profound commitment to record events in their individual substance, no longer regimenting them in majestic sequences or a priori full-and-empty balances. Taking their cue from this popular idiom, the Arts and Crafts masters and their disciples, from Charles Robert Ashbee to Charles F. Annesley Voysey, worked out a vocabulary which, within a few years, completely supplanted every figurative remnant of the same Middle Ages.

—dialogue between structure and shell. Constructions where "stone components and walls formed a single unit" strongly ap-

---

100–1. The listing method in the medieval Piazza San Pellegrino of Viterbo (thirteenth century) and in "The Pastures" house at North Luffenham, designed by Charles F. Annesley Voysey in 1901. Voysey's work concluded the Arts and Crafts cycle initiated in 1859 with William Morris' Red House (cf. 44). The Morris reform opposed neoclassicism and its dogmas: symmetry, proportion, rhythm, full-and-empty balance, aligned doors and windows, and the monumental. It strove for a descriptive language of functions and natural materials which, eliminating the Renaissance orders, or "set phrases," gave new semantic value to every architectural "word."

pealed to the neo-Romanesque architects determined to cast off programmatic Gothic and neo-Gothic anatomical structuralism. Hendrik Petrus Berlage's Stock Exchange in Amsterdam echoes Sant'Ambrogio in Milan. On the heavy Lombard walls, full of deep shadows, the struts and ribs of the crossings are visible but do not contrast with the brick texture. Similarly, in the Netherlands, iron framings cover a luminous space enclosed by robust neo-Romanesque walls and connect with them by indented truss members that disappear into the masonry.

Exposing the structural frame was a medieval lesson that went beyond Arts and Crafts and the neo-Romanesque movement. Frank Lloyd Wright, fervent medievalist, used this approach in his Hickox House (1900) in Kankakee, first step in his crusade to do away with the "box" and to conceive walls as mere screens in the continuum between inside and outside spaces. Ludwig Mies van der Rohe followed suit with obsessive modularity in his Illinois Institute of Technology (1940–56) in Chicago.

The Arts and Crafts leaders, from Morris to Voysey, and the neo-Romanesques, from Henry Hobson Richardson and John Wellborn Root to Berlage, fomented a trend, soon spread throughout the world, to rid architecture of spurious classical precepts. Even in Italy, stronghold of academism, such men as Boito, Ernesto Basile, and Gaetano Moretti gave it their full support. Artists with creative imagination and indomitable courage abandoned the archaeological neomedievalism of the nineteenth-century romantics. They were truly modern poets who mirrored their anxieties in the past. They built and studied, created and explored, impelled by a passion for the new that drove them to "excavate"

102–4. Romanesque and neo-Romanesque. *Above:* two views of the cross vaults in Sant'Ambrogio, Milan (second half of the eleventh century). *Below:* Hall of the Amsterdam Stock Exchange (1898), by Hendrik Petrus Berlage, whose cultural role in Europe paralleled that of Henry Hobson Richardson in the United States (cf. 42, 95, and 96).
Following page:
105–6. Exposed timber framework in the Cloister Court of Queen's College, Cambridge (1448), and exposed metal framework in the Alumni Memorial Hall of the Illinois Institute of Technology, Chicago (1945), by Ludwig Mies van der Rohe.

buried erudition and bring it back to life. They spoke in terms of today and reread the past with modern eyes.

Their permanent contribution to the contemporary language of architecture lies in functional listing as design methodology. They did away with both grammar and syntax, rules and dogma, to revive the semantics of words that had lost their true meaning in the conventional phrases coined by the "orders," by their super-impositions and juxtapositions, consonances and proportions. The list, or inventory of functions, constitutes the basic invariable of the modern language in architecture: unless he rejects the ta-boos and the abstract, coercive precepts of classicism, no man can be a modern architect. Thus, the medieval experience still offers today the best instrument for shaping a cultured and, at the same time, popular language, for determining its matrix and controlling its development.

Preceding pages:
107. Aerial view of abbey of Mont-Saint-Michel (1022–1135).
Above:
108. The Eiffel Tower (1889), dominating the panorama of Paris.
Following pages:
109–10. Structural prodigies. *Left:* vaults over the choir of the cathedral of Amiens (1220–47). *Right:* Galerie des Machines, by Victor Contamin and Charles-Louis-Ferdinand Dutert, built for the Paris Exhibition of 1889. Its dimensions: length, 1,377 feet; width, 377 feet; height, 157 feet high.

IX

Gothic Historiography, Nineteenth-Century Engineering,
Art Nouveau, Garden Cities: Asymmetry and Dissonance;
Cantilever, Shell, and Membrane Structures

The Gothic revival, pioneered by the Frenchman Eugène Viollet-le-Duc (1814–79), preceded the neo-Romanesque. Richardson rebelled against the Beaux-Arts school's tendency to crystallize fourteenth-century forms into a "style," and Berlage followed P. J. H. Cuypers, who designed the Rijksmuseum (1877), Amsterdam, in the Gothic manner. Moreover, the Arts and Crafts movement came long after the birth of modern engineering. William Morris' Red House was built in 1859, while the first iron bridge, at Coalbrookdale, England, dates back to 1775. Nevertheless, as a parameter for a renewed language, the Gothic culture prevailed during the last decades of the nineteenth century. This may be demonstrated by comparing two celebrated strongholds of the new technique. The Crystal Palace (1851) in London marked a long forward stride in structural evolution, but its ornamental tracery and Second Empire arabesques were weak and ineffectual. Inversely, the Galerie des Machines (1889) at the Paris World Exhibition of 1889 embodied Viollet-le-Duc's principles, but stripped them of every archaeological encumbrance.

What features of the Gothic culture attracted modern artists? There are many, some of them contradictory, including:

—structural framework. Steel and reinforced concrete concentrated weights and stresses into isolated supports, thus eliminating the continuous substaining wall. Immediate, inevitable historical antecedents of this development were the cathedrals of the Ile de France, from Notre Dame to Amiens, which illustrate the progressive atrophy of walls. Vertical elements began to scan volumes and spaces. Between them, immense, luminous openwork

made it possible to pare down the traditionally heavy walls to thin screens. Innumerable modern buildings, such as Alfred Messel's Wertheim Department Store in Berlin, follow the same approach.

—transparency. At its apex, Gothic architecture provoked a typical fascinating effect: the brilliant light streaming through the air-borne dust inundated the building envelope and nullified the feeling of a boxlike mass. Thus, external and internal spaces seemed to merge together, and the framework looked much like a cage, with its sheer lines traced against the sky. Seeking to recapture this magical dream and struck by the infinite possibilities offered by iron and glass, nineteenth-century engineers split the landscape into soaring segments, almost measuring the unlimited space. Subsequently, Auguste Perret introduced geometric fretwork in the churches of Le Raincy and Montmagny, and Lloyd Wright, son of the Taliesin genius, built a crystal chapel (1951) at Palos Verdes, California.

—dynamic lines. The composite pilasters of the cathedrals and the sharply projecting cornices of the fourteenth-century palaces were invested with a linear dynamism, which Art Nouveau revived. Line is strength, said Henry van de Velde, whose restless, writhing designs were conceived in terms of *Einfühlung*, that is, in a physiopsychological function. This concept Victor Horta had already grasped in his house on the Rue de Turin (1893), Brussels. Stripping away the stone trappings with which the academics dressed their iron columns, he left them bare and extended their lines in vivid, ornamental motives.

Preceding pages:
111–12. The structural skeleton. *Left:* rampant arches of the cathedral of Chartres (1194–1220). *Right:* refinery in Texas (1937).
Facing page:
113–14. Transparency. *Above:* rose window of the transept in Notre Dame de Paris (1163–1220). *Below:* insets in reinforced concrete, designed by Auguste Perret, in Notre Dame at Le Raincy (1922).
Following pages:
115–17. Transparency. Sainte-Chapelle in Paris (1246–48). Interior and side view of the chapel at Palos Verdes, California (1951), by Lloyd Wright, son of the Taliesin master.

118–19. Dynamic lines. The nave of the Wells Cathedral (1192–1230) and the glass vault of the winter garden in the house built by Victor Horta on Avenue Palmerston, Brussels (1895). At its outset, Art Nouveau reverted to the Gothic in order to free the new iron structures of classical constraints, and prolonged the optical thrust of columns and beams in wriggling ornamental inventions that animated the entire spatial form. Horta could make even a stone vibrate, as shown by the ventilating apertures in his studio at Saint-Gilles, Brussels (cf. 43), and in many details of the Maison du Peuple, his masterwork (cf. 13).

—shells and membranes. In the fifteenth and sixteenth centuries, Gothic architecture subdued the dynamic tension, preferring more complex interlacing often unrelated to the structures themselves. In England, we find the vaulted texture of the King's College Chapel in Cambridge. The umbrellalike tracery of the Canterbury Cathedral replaced the sprouting pilasters of Salisbury. An image free of dynamic impulses was produced in the vibrating, yet static, lines of the Bodleian Library in Oxford. Such emancipation from the technical data brought about two consequences. The first, more evident, was negative. Despite its masterpieces, the late Gothic was so obsessed with intellectual refinements that it deteriorated more than once into the merely decorative. The same fate befell Art Nouveau centuries later when it abandoned Horta's startling lines and van de Velde's functional precepts, only to waste away into the excesses of floral art. This was the case of Joseph Hoffmann. In 1905 this Viennese architect discovered the secret of the thin, tortile columns at the corners of the Ducal Palace in Venice: they speed up the refractions of light and separate the volumetric surfaces, thus dissembling their thickness. These properties Hoffman adapted to the bronzed profiles of the Palais Stoclet in Brussels, thereby uniting the most dissonant elements. But in the Austrian Pavilion at the 1934 Venice Biennale, he made a half-hearted effort to add tension to a symmetrical volume designed in the classical manner, with quivering, corrugated sheathing. The second consequence of the late Gothic approach, however, is positive and significant for today's architects: omitting the dynamic lines, membranes and shells reintegrated the building envelope. Similarly, the most advanced modern structures do not separate the supports from the intermediate sectors, but rather involve every fiber of the organism in the

120–21. Linear virtuosity. Late Gothic devitalized the dynamic concept with a decorative style exemplified in the church of Santa Barbara at Kuttenberg (1512). Art Nouveau reached a similar stage, as shown by the railings for the Paris Métro, designed by Hector Guimard in 1900.

Following pages:

122–23. Membranes and linear shells in King's College Chapel, Cambridge (1446–1515), and a geodesic cupola built by Buckminster Fuller for the American Pavilion at the Montreal Exhibition of 1967. "Hippy" domes followed his example (cf. 223 and 224).

Above:
124. A weft of lines over the façade of the Bodleian Library in Oxford (1613–18).

Facing page:
125–28. *Left:* the tortile column at the corner of the Palazzo Ducale in Venice (twelfth to fifteenth centuries). *Right:* two views of the bronzed seams that frame the façades of the Palais Stoclet, Brussels (1905–11), by Joseph Hoffmann, and divide them into bidimensional sectors. *Below:* Hoffmann's Austrian Pavilion at the Venice Biennale of 1934. The corrugated surface harks back to the Viennese Art Nouveau master's sensitivity, but the symmetry of the building indicates his creative decline.

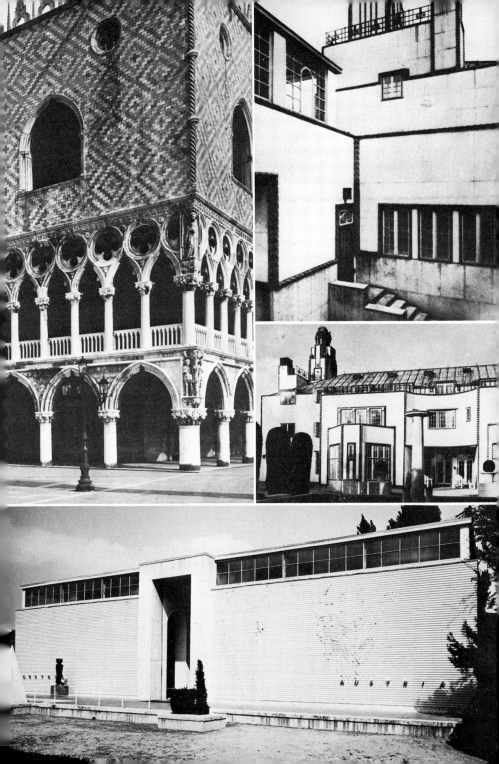

molded forms. We see examples of this in Pier Luigi Nervi's cupolas.

—undulating surfaces. Whenever the Gothic spatial continuum could not make use of dynamic lines and broad glass expanses, architects curved exterior walls to temper severe, heavy stereometries. The town halls of Perugia and Siena were designed in this way to be sensitized to the light, and keep their crenellated summits in permanent interaction with the surrounding atmosphere. Art Nouveau, too, abhorred harsh geometric surfaces: the entire façade of Horta's Maison du Peuple in Brussels is concave. John Root used bow windows on the Monadnock Block in Chicago to relieve the otherwise monotonous rigidity of that giant pile in a play of interruptions.

—the vertical. Height is the symbol of mystic and human prestige. The industrialists of the nineteenth century sought to compensate for the religious crisis with the cult of money and free enterprise. The tower of Bruges, the Strasbourg Cathedral, and Mont-Saint-Michel, designed to emphasize and exalt the church spire rising high above the town, exemplify the transcendency of medieval verticalism. Among the corresponding modern structures, we can cite Alessandro Antonelli's works in Turin and Novara; Gustave Eiffel's famous Tower (1889) in Paris, which dominates the city; and America's soaring skyscrapers, varying in type from the neo-Gothic, such as the Woolworth Building in New York, to the rationalist masterpiece by George Howe and William Lescaze, the Philadelphia Savings Fund Society Building. Frank Lloyd Wright, who declared that his work was "conceived in the Gothic spirit" when he introduced it to Europe in 1910, designed Broadacre City, a horizontal habitat, but also "The Illinois," a mile-high skyscraper.

129–31. Undulating surfaces. The Palazzo Comunale in Perugia (thirteenth to fourteenth centuries), by Giacomo di Servadio and Giovannello di Benvenuto. Monadnock Building in Chicago (1891), by John Root and Daniel Burnham. The concave front of the Maison du Peuple in Brussels (1896–99), by Victor Horta. *Following pages:*
132–33. The vertical. Tower of the Bruges Town Hall (end of the thirteenth century) and "The Illinois," mile-high skyscraper designed for Chicago by Frank Lloyd Wright in 1956. See also 107 for Mont-Saint-Michel, and 108 for the Eiffel Tower.

—asymmetry and dissonance. The striking dissimilarities between the two towers of the Chartres Cathedral; the "early English," "decorated," and "perpendicular" chapels audaciously matched in Great Britain's churches; and the notorious imbalance of Arnolfo di Cambio's Palazzo Vecchio tower in Florence showed a strong attraction for asymmetry and dissonance, cardinal invariables of the modern language of architecture. Indeed, the Gothic formulated a methodology of dissonance when, superseding the one-dimensional scheme of the Christian basilica, it exacerbated the contrast between the longitudinal distance to the altar and the visual distance to the cross vaults at vertiginous heights overhead. Moreover, abbeys and monasteries, especially in England, were seldom completed. They constantly grew and added new quarters, but no effort was made to endow them all with a uniform style. Indeed, their differences were often accentuated to a surrealistic degree.

The influence of medieval town planning on modern planning goes beyond a visual and symbolic comparison. In 1889, Camillo Sitte published *Der Städtebau nach seinen Künstlerischen Grundsätzen,* a sort of glorification of urban art in the Middle Ages. Nine years later, Ebenezer Howard, embalming the nineteenth-century utopias of Robert Owen and Charles Fourier, wrote *Tomorrow: A Peaceful Path to Real Reform,* which became the gospel of the new town planning movement. The notion of the Garden City found immediate historical reference to those centuries "when cathedrals were white" and the network of European settlements was planned with reckless fantasy and courage.

Howard deplored the hypertrophic expansion of metropolitan areas, calling instead for satellite communities of about thirty

---

134–35. Asymmetry and dissonance. Spires of unequal height (377 and 347 feet) of the cathedral of Chartres (1194–1220). Dissonant volumes in Rockefeller Center, New York (1931–39), by Hood & Fouilhoux, Reinhard & Hofmeister, Corbett, Harrison & MacMurray.
Following pages:
136–37. Gothic and modern dissonance. A twisted column in the church of Saint-Severin, Paris (fifteenth century), and model of the Palace of the Third International in Moscow, designed by Vladimir Tatlin in 1920. The helicoidal form of this building signaled a rupture with the static box of the classicist idiom.

thousand inhabitants, economically and functionally autonomous. At the same time, Sitte praised the medieval nuclei for
their limited size, their asymmetrical squares and streets, and their
dissonant monuments. Sociology, artistic creativity, and architectural history combined to shape the idea of Letchworth and
Welwyn Garden Cities, the workers' communities designed by
Bruno Taut and Ernst May, Sabaudia near Rome, the American
"greenbelts," and finally the New Towns in Great Britain and
Scandinavia—in short, everything positive that was realized in
town planning until the advent of an alternative hypothesis: the
city-region.

138–40. The community dimension. *Above:* New Lanark, near Glasgow, one of
Britain's first workers' centers, built by Robert Owen in 1802. *Right:* aerial views
of Lucignano, a medieval Tuscan agglomerate, and Bram, near Carcassonne.
Following pages:
141–42. *Left:* aerial view of Perugia (cf. 94). *Right:* aerial view of Welwyn Garden
City, second such community realized, through the initiative of Ebenezer Howard,
by Louis de Soissons and Arthur Kenyon (1919). The British and Scandinavian
satellite towns are an outgrowth of the Garden City concept, formulated by Howard at the end of the last century.

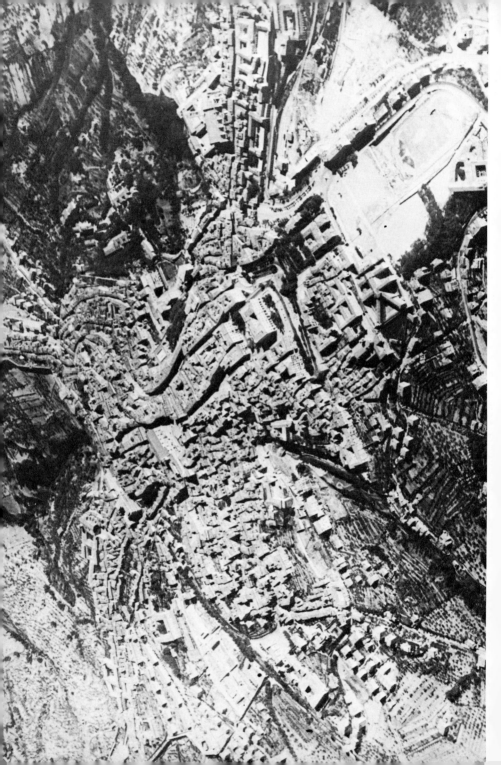

Preceding pages:
143. The Renaissance decomposing method of design (nave, vaults, ring, cupola, lantern) in the church of Santa Maria delle Carceri in Prato (1485), by Giuliano da Sangallo.
Above:
144. Neoplastic decomposing in a chair by Gerrit Rietveld, exponent of the De Stijl Group (1922).
Following pages:
145–46. Renaissance proportions in a drawing by Leonardo da Vinci, and the Modulor worked out by Le Corbusier in 1947.

X

Renaissance and Rationalism: Antiperspective Three-Dimensionality, Syntax of Four-dimensional Decomposition

A close scrutiny of past records will confirm beyond all doubt that historical commitment and architectural creativity are interdependent. No link seems to bind the Renaissance revival, fostered, among others, by Jacob Burckhardt in his *Die Kultur der Renaissance in Italien* (1880), with the modern rationalism of the 1920s and 1930s. The last vestiges of a Renaissance indoctrination can be found in the works of the Austrian Otto Wagner, although he repudiated it in his *Moderne Architektur* (1895), in the output of Karl Friedrich Schinkel's followers, and, to a very limited extent, in Tony Garnier's project for "Une cité industrielle," dated 1901–4.

Nevertheless, anyone who maintains that modern rationalism preserves classicist elements—Beaux-Arts in reverse—because of its muddle-headed aim to devise a universally applicable code founded on rigid standards puts his finger on a basic question. The commerce between past culture and contemporary architecture is a dynamic one. It is effective even when hidden behind a screen of dialectic contradictions. Let us consider the generic analogies that link twentieth-century rationalism to the Renaissance:

—a drastic reduction of linguistic instruments. From the formal anthology of the Middle Ages, Brunelleschi selected only a very few elements. He would have nothing to do with marble inlays, chromatic hedonism, volumetric elasticity, fussy walls, pointed arches, composite pilasters, structural ostentation, or Gothic asymmetry and dissonance. Omitting every chance intrusion, he distilled a lean vocabulary stripped of all such adjectives. In the

171

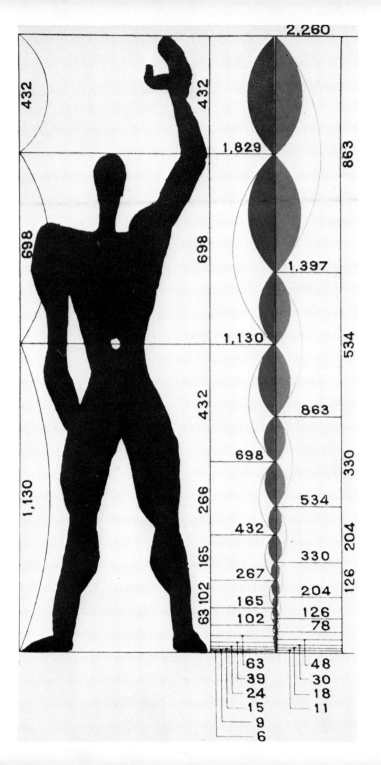

post-World War I years, Le Corbusier, Gropius, Mies van der Rohe, and J. J. P. Oud did the same; in a parallel move, stoutly professing to be artists with no need for such expedients, they made a clean sweep of romantic Eclecticism, Art Nouveau, and the protorationalism that prevailed between 1900 and 1914. Just as Brunelleschi had turned his back on the Gothic line, they refused floral decoration. They were inflexibly simple, and their luminous volumes stood out in the architectural scene for the deliberate paucity of the means employed.

—scientific ideology and intellectual control. The discovery of perspective underlay Renaissance poetics in the same way that the Cubists' discovery of the fourth dimension provided the basis for modern rationalism. The myth of perfect proportion, the application of the golden section, the longing to hit on some method of design that would be valid for any theme whatever, as well as a didactic mentality united the architectural cycle of the twenties and thirties to the Renaissance. In both cases, poetry was oriented toward mathematics.

—elementary geometry and stereometry. The plan of Le Corbusier's Villa Savoye is a square, as are the bays of Brunelleschi's portico of the Ospedale degli Innocenti in Florence. Oud's workers' housing in Rotterdam has circular street corners, and the centric system was the Renaissance humanistic ideal. "Pure" shapes exposed to the light, and therefore immediately legible, replace the incommensurable values and elaborate patterns of the preceding periods. Santa Maria della Consolazione in Todi is a rippling image of spheres and cylinders, isolated from nature. Le Corbusier's prisms, resting on pilotis, widen the breach.

147–48. Elementary geometry. Circles, cylinders, and spheres in Rotterdam's low-cost housing project, by J. J. P. Oud (1924), and in the church of Santa Maria della Consolazione in Todi, by Cola di Matteuccio di Caprarola (1508–12).
Following pages:
149–51. Proportional relationships in the Palazzo Bartolini, Florence, by Baccio d'Agnolo (beginning of the sixteenth century) and in two works by Le Corbusier: Ozenfant's studio house in Paris (1922) and Maison La Roche in Auteuil, designed in 1923 (cf. 39). The search for the "golden section" was common to both the Renaissance and the rationalist movement between the two world wars.

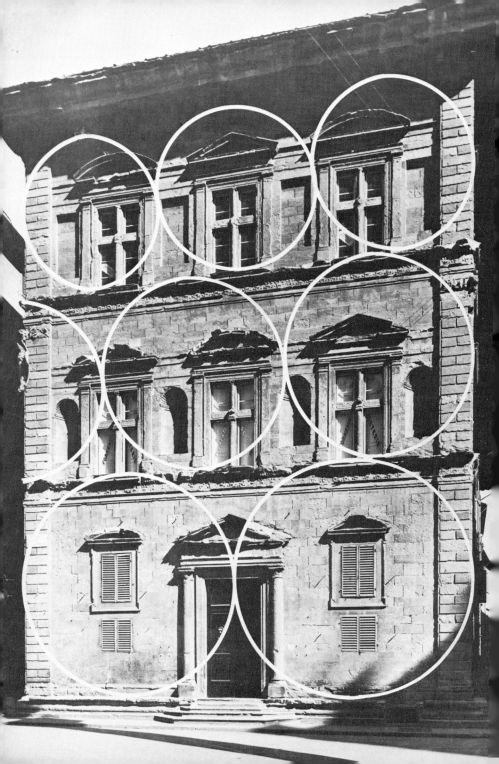

These analogies stem from a similar process of dismembering spatial organisms, volumes, planes, and surfaces. Brunelleschi began to decompose with his very first work, the portico of the Innocenti. Did the plan call for a rectangle? He split it up into a series of squares. What about the elevation? He chose a module, an arch over a square, and repeated it along the length of the façade. He was called upon to design a stone façade for the Palazzo Pitti, a theme with a glorious unitarian tradition in medieval architecture, brightened by a variety of apertures and dynamic lines. But he disintegrated the whole by selecting a window module and repeating it seven times horizontally, then following the same method vertically and decomposing the height into three equal parts. What was called the Renaissance "superimposition of the orders" arose from this syntax of decomposition, applied in two or three dimensions. Examples: the courtyard of the Cancelleria in Rome and the interior of Santa Maria delle Carceri in Prato. Even the voids are disassembled into separate entities—the main nave, secondary naves, transept, pendentives, drum, cupola, lantern, and summit—then juxtaposed or superposed, but nowhere fused together.

From this architectural code came the need for proportion. No law must govern the elements of medieval buildings; the functional listing possessed inner corrective capacities within a narrative approach. Renaissance decomposition, on the other hand, demanded a whole series of rules. How often could the hollow module of the Innocenti be repeated? Should the Palazzo Pitti have seven windows or ten? Could the spans of San Lorenzo in Florence be undefined or must they conform to a stern mathematical edict? How would the Palazzo Bartolini in Florence have

---

152–53. Modular composition in the seven central windows of the Palazzo Pitti in Florence, by Filippo Brunelleschi (1440), and in the Berlin-Dahlem housing project designed by Wassili and Hans Luckhardt and Alfons Anker during the rationalist period (1928). Classicism, ancient and modern, proceeds by modules and repeats them systematically, contravening the invariable of functional listing which constitutes the basis of a democratic language. Windows and living cells are uniformly repeated, obeying the academic canons. Architectural "words" lose their specific semantics in deference to the "orders."

turned out had its composition been altered even slightly? Otherwise stated, if you decompose the whole into modules, how do you close the sequence of the modules, how do you make it clear that a building ends at such-and-such a point, not before and not beyond? It is here that proportion played its role and, with it, the eurhythmics, the golden number, the pseudoscientific baggage of consonance, and the expediency of balustrades, friezes, cymae, cornucopias, lacunars, cornices, tiles, trusses, and escutcheons, which strengthen or weaken the visual weight of the elements bearing on the proportional rhythms.

Translating the same process into dynamic terms, let us look at the architecture of the 1920s and 1930s. Expressionism did not decompose but gave to its three-dimensional masses an explosive kinetic tension, that is, antiperspective and contrary to the Renaissance procedure. Architectural trends influenced by Cubism, however, preferred to decompose the building box into dissonant volumes. Neoplasticism, the De Stijl movement led by Theo van Doesburg, expounded the four-dimensional syntax by dismembering the volume into free slabs, then reassembling them, but in such a way as to avoid the static perspective vision. De Stijl hailed the fourth dimension—time—as the crowning glory of architectural enjoyment. Poet laureate of this tendency was Mies van der Rohe, who eliminated every closed binding of spaces and used a single instrument—the isolated slab—for walls, ceilings, reflector pools, marble sheets, or glass to mark out spatial fluidity. Another significant artist was Robert Maillart, a modest Swiss engineer who was unaware of his exceptional stature. Dismissing structural exhibitionism, he designed his famous bridges in simple slabs of reinforced concrete. More sophisticated, Gerrit

---

154–56. Renaissance perspective and Expressionist antiperspective three-dimensionality. Piazza della Santissima Annunziata in Florence (cf. 169), with the church flanked by Brunelleschi's portico and by a sixteenth-century copy of it in the foreground. Two sketches for the Alexanderplatz in Berlin, by the Luckhardt brothers, who used the Expressionist innovations introduced during the early post-World War I period (1929). For centuries, central perspective suppressed the three-dimensionality of the urban fabric. The Expressionists vindicated it in an anti-Renaissance key, while De Stijl aimed for four-dimensional decomposition.

Rietveld adopted decomposition even in his chairs, breaking up traditional forms into small elements, then combining them, but openly exposing the procedure of their assemblage.

The rationalist taste for pure volumes parallels the Renaissance need for decomposing the urban continuum typical of the Middle Ages: no more streets like canals flanked by rows of houses, no more squares like so many cubes of air marked off by classical buildings, like so many stage sets. The "free plan," throwing off the ball and chain of perspective, is the dominating principle of the modern vision. It is valuable to city spaces as well as to interiors.

The fourth dimension, therefore, takes a militant stand against the three-dimensional inflexibility of classicism, replacing the static (one fixed viewpoint giving one fixed perspective image) with movement (infinite viewpoints with as many images). But the Renaissance and modern rationalism share a theoretical and analytical anguish so closely that the old and new romantics denounce the intellectual furbelows of both, their pseudological nightmares and the icy, catechistic limits of their imagination. The romantics fail to see the magic of the number and the intoxicating mystique in the dream of golden mean or of four-dimensional dissonance.

157–60. The Renaissance three-dimensional and the modern four-dimensional. *Upper left:* the module of the Ospedale degli Innocenti in Florence (cf. 154), by Brunelleschi (1419). *Upper right and center:* two views of the German Pavilion at the Barcelona Exhibition of 1929, by Ludwig Mies van der Rohe. *Below:* bridge over the Tschiel-Bach Valley in Switzerland, by Robert Maillart (1925).

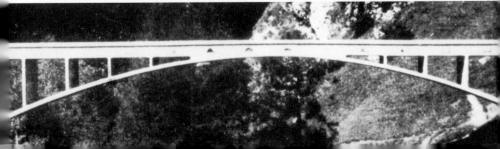

XI

Mannerism and Baroque, Organic Architecture: Space in Time; Reintegration of Building, City, and Landscape

Through the mediation of Mannerism, which broke down Renaissance classical ideologies by dismantling their structure of proportions and relationships, the transition to the Baroque brought reintegration with it. An analogous role was played by the organic movement, both in the direction taken by Frank Lloyd Wright after the rationalism of the Chicago School of 1880–93, and in the European development centering on Alvar Aalto, Scandinavian Neo-Empiricism, and the Neo-Expressionist currents in the post-World War II period. Mannerism and Baroque intersected in the sixteenth and seventeenth centuries; likewise, in modern times, Brutalism, a Manneristic phenomenon, followed the organic. Le Corbusier's work embodied all three phases. Standard bearer of rationalism in the 1920s and 1930s, he abandoned it when he designed the Ronchamp chapel with strong Baroque overtones. In the La Tourette monastery near Lyons, however, and in his constructions in Chandigarh, he consolidated "manner."

In the outcry against the canons of classicism, the voice of Michelangelo resounded above all others. The stairway in the Laurentian Library, Florence, bursts upward through the hall with explosive force. Immense twin columns, embedded in the walls and seemingly struggling to free themselves, apostrophize the white surface, marked by regularly spaced sixteenth-century modules. And the cascading steps contrast strikingly with the insipid void, in an expressionist complaint against the aseptic balance of spaces.

In the palaces of the Campidoglio in Rome, Michelangelo reintegrated volume, emphasizing its total height with gigantic

pillars. Called upon to complete the Palazzo Farnese, he brushed aside the cautious design by Sangallo and added a colossal cornice, fully disproportionate because it relates not with the third order but with the entire façade (the apparently similar impressive cornice of the Early Renaissance Palazzo Strozzi in Florence floats on a smooth separating strip, in harmony with the tripartition of the ashlar box below). Furthermore, Michelangelo defied the Renaissance code with his sweeping designs for the fortifications of Florence. As with the Capitoline complex, he replaced symmetry—and a lack of tension—with a compressed trapezoidal void and gave dynamic force to the piazza by inverting the perspective alignment. In the apse of St. Peter's and at the Porta Pia, he went not only beyond Mannerism but beyond Baroque as well.

Carrying forward a parallel function, modern Expressionism stirred up a dramatic controversy against the principle of decomposition and in favor of reintegration. Its foremost exponents were Antoni Gaudí in Spain and Erich Mendelsohn in Germany. Numerous works, such as Rudolf Steiner's Goetheanum in Dornach, near Basel, bear eloquent witness to the exuberance of its flowing, plastic forms. In Barcelona, the contorted façade of Gaudí's Milá House introduced asymmetries never seen before; its phantasmagoric, modeled contours confound the sky with a series of gesticulating totems, and its interior spaces seem like hollowed-out lumps of clay. The Einstein Observatory in Potsdam, bristling with protuberances and undulations, bursts out of the earth like a volcano in eruption. In a spectral scenography, Otto Bartning reunified the exotic, forestlike elements of a sanctuary, weakening them by using pendulous shapes.

167–73. The antidecomposing controversy provoked by Michelangelo and again, centuries later, by the Expressionists. Palazzo Farnese in Rome (1546) with its immense cornice which unifies the superimposed orders. The trapezoidal layout of the Piazza del Campidoglio, Rome, compared with the perspective plan of the Piazza della Santissima Annunziata in Florence (cf. 154). Sketch by Michelangelo for the Florence fortifications of 1529 (cf. 26–28). *Below:* Einstein Tower in Potsdam, by Erich Mendelsohn (1920), and project for a church by Otto Bartning (1921), two examples of Expressionism that reintegrate the elements decomposed through the analytical methodology of rationalism.

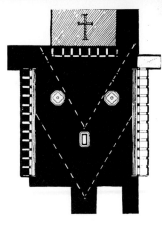
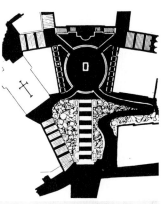

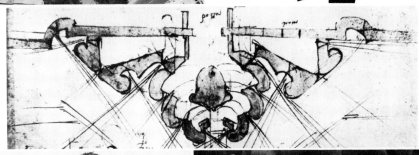

Introducing powerful dynamics in perspective vision and temporizing the three-dimensional, this revolutionary movement ruled out as superfluous both the fourth dimension and the decomposing method of two-dimensional planes and slabs. But a process of reintegration also affected the language deriving from Cubism. In the pavilions of the Stockholm Exhibition of 1930, Erik Gunnar Asplund waived the laws of prismatic rigidity and the strictures of the T-square in favor of sinuous fluidity and curves, which promoted a continuing interaction between volumes.

Let us now analyze the church of the Gesù in Rome. Here the method of decomposing, in the syntactical sense, still survives. The whole is dismembered into the principal nave, rows of chapels, presbytery, transept, cupola, and apse. If, however, we compare it with a fifteenth-century model—even with its exceptional predecessor, Sant'Andrea in Mantua—we shall understand the crisis that beleaguered Renaissance conceptions. The atrophy of the Gesù's minor naves, replaced by chapels, and the encapsulation of the transept into a cubic volume give full pre-eminence to the central space, which dominates the interior as the cynosure of the total image. The passage from harmonic and equivalent modules to a hierarchic vision brought with it—as Heinrich Wölfflin amply demonstrated in his *Renaissance und Barok* (1888)— a reunification of the fragments from the preceding culture, their reintegration. A minor Renaissance nave forms an autonomous perspective image. In Sant'Andrea, too, we find a spatial articulation, whereas the Gesù chapels are entirely secondary to the single majestic nave. Let us compare the cupola of this Roman church with Santa Maria delle Carceri in Prato, to take an example. Here

---

174–76. *Above:* Erik Gunnar Asplund's pavilions at the Stockholm Exhibition of 1930, a criticism of the rationalist decomposition of volumes. *Center:* plans of San Lorenzo in Florence, by Brunelleschi (1423); Sant'Andrea in Mantua, by Leon Battista Alberti (1470); and the church of the Gesù in Rome, by Jacopo Barozzi da Vignola (1568). *Below:* cupola of the Gesù by Vignola and Giacomo Della Porta (1568–73). By reducing the lateral naves to chapels, the Gesù opposes the traditional tripartitioning of the Christian church and introduces the question of reintegration, subsequently resolved in the Baroque period.

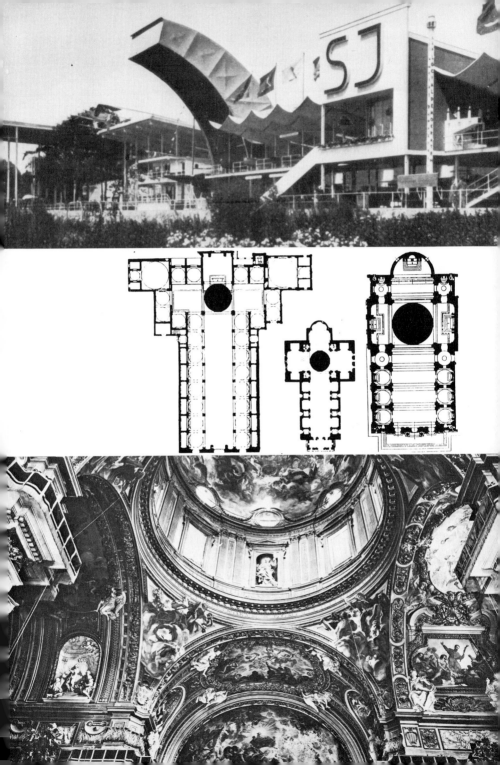

we find the same decomposing process, in the mechanical sense: archivolts that define the barrel vaults of the nave and transept, and a drum resting on a ring. Yet, the differences are striking. The Baroque decoration blends the elements together, while in Prato the vaults, lunettes, and shining segments accentuate the separation. The ring in Prato is markedly detached from the side cornices, while the one in Gesù tends to become fused. More important, in Rome the diameter of the enormous cupola matches the width of the nave. Overwhelming in its magnitude, it is antagonistic to the eurhythmic laws of the Renaissance since it ignores consonances and proportion.

As Vignola did in the Gesù, so Aalto boycotted decomposition in his library at Viipuri. A wooden ceiling undulates over the rectangular assembly room and extends down to the floor, covering its backdrop wall. Instead of dismembering the box into six slabs, Aalto achieved a unity of ceiling and wall. His approach is manneristic, it confutes rationalism from within through an organic device that would subsequently influence space concepts.

To return to the Baroque: an aversion to the static was the natural consequence of a determination to reintegrate. The elliptical plan, which even such a hesitant artist as Bernini used repeatedly, dissociates space into two focuses, giving each element a double reference. Since the eye is spontaneously drawn from one focus to the other, the vision becomes kinetic. In Santa Maria in Campitelli, Rome, Carlo Rainaldi took a more audacious risk by arranging two contiguous spaces along a longitudinal axis. Not content with this duality, he fused the two spaces together through a play of plasticism, intensified at the point where they join. This expedient, however, still failed to satisfy him. Therefore, since the far chamber provides a sort of proscenium for the first

---

177–81. *Above:* Conference room in the Viipuri Library, by Alvar Aalto (1930–35), with its undulating "Mannerist" wood ceiling, which descends to cover the wall behind the speaker's area. *Center:* Cupola and ellipsoidal plan of Sant'Andrea al Quirinale, Rome, by Gian Lorenzo Bernini (1658). *Below:* view and plan of Santa Maria in Campitelli, Rome, by Carlo Rainaldi (1657), with its two chambers juxtaposed longitudinally. Here reintegration is achieved through the contrast between a large dark chamber and an adjoining one brilliantly illuminated from the cupola.

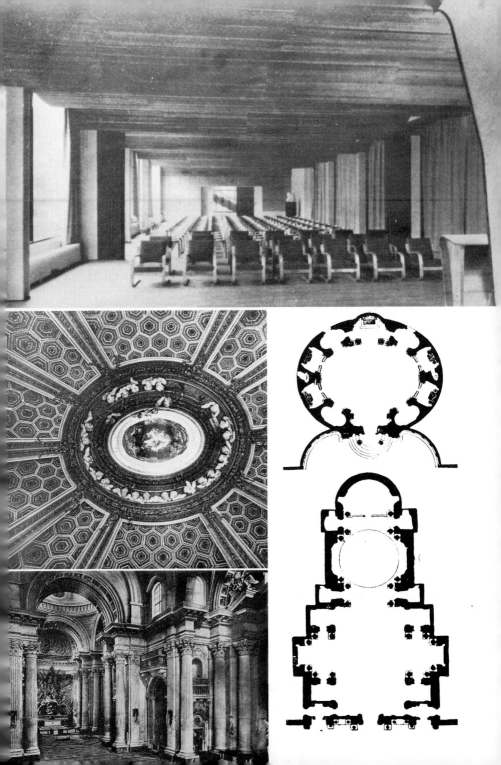

and does not draw the visitor to it, Rainaldi gave the two spaces unequal light values: the first chamber is dark, while the second is filled with dazzling luminosity. Thus he complemented a dimensional dissonance with a dissonance of light.

Similarly, Le Corbusier studded the wall of the Ronchamp chapel with holes of different sizes and shapes to achieve a brilliant, arcane lighting effect.

The interpenetration of spatial figures culminated with Borromini and provided a stimulus for structural continuity. This was his unequivocal choice, beginning with the church of San Carlino alle Quattro Fontane. The space he had to work with was extremely narrow, and this would ordinarily call for a rectangular plan. Such a plan, however, was not acceptable, because it implied decomposing into the facade wall, the side walls, and the far wall. A circle? This would have resulted in static uniformity. An oval? Too simple. It would have defied classicism without disposing of it. Borromini's solution was highly complex: two pairs of ellipses, partially overlapping to form a configuration which shapes a tortuous mural band. One cannot grasp the whole from any single viewing point, as a constant movement is infused in this minimal, yet unconfined, space.

The genetics of Sant'Agnese in the Piazza Navona, Rome, can be traced in three stages:

—act one: the pre-existent church, an ineffective, almost longitudinal scheme;

—act two: the initial plan, recalling Michelangelo's idea for St. Peter's. A cupola dominates and compresses the structure below it, with an explosive proportional dissonance over a Renaissance double symmetry;

---

182. Dissonance of light marking the two chambers of Santa Maria in Campitelli, Rome, by Carlo Rainaldi (cf. 180 and 181). *At the right,* the first dark chamber, entered from the piazza; *at the left,* the small chamber inundated with light polarized on the altar.
183. Wall studded with light-admitting apertures in Le Corbusier's Chapelle de Notre-Dame du Haut at Ronchamp (1950–51). For other views of this chapel, see 79 and 80. The quantitative and qualitative diversification of light reintegrates the architectural space and temporizes the spectator's vision of it. This diversification was used in the Baroque and in the postrationalist periods.

—act three: the final plan, both dilated and contracted, uncontainable within a perspective image, an immense broken profile that temporizes the space. Let us examine the relationship between church and cupola. As we enter the building, the widest vertical visual angle includes the cornice below the drum. Measuring Borromini's section, we see that it is barely halfway up the astonishing height. This incredible "disproportion" does not allow us to view the whole from any one position. We must move about and take time to grasp its dramatic message. The Baroque brings the object closer to the observer so that he will not mistake it as something detached, something only to contemplate. The interior of Sant'Agnese draws him into its vortex; to appreciate it, he must "live" it actively.

Leaping over the centuries to modern architecture, we have seen how Asplund's "Mannerism" provoked the crisis of volumetric decomposition, and Aalto's postulated a reintegration in the rationalist prism in Viipuri. The Finnish Pavilion at the New York World's Fair of 1939 corresponded to Sant'Agnese. Instead of dividing its quadrangular volume into slabs, Aalto compressed the space with a cyclopic corrugated wall, in a gesture reminiscent of Michelangelo. He suppressed every horizontal perspective image, then divided the height into four sections. The lower one is bottomless, while the other three above it impend on the observer, catching him in rough, turgid, overflowing forms that replace the diaphanous surfaces and the precise contours of four-dimensional rationalism.

The saga of cupolas reached its conclusion with the prodigious church of Sant'Ivo alla Sapienza, in Rome. It gave the coup de grâce to the Renaissance and Manneristic decomposition method,

---

184–86. Plan of Sant'Agnese in the Piazza Navona, Rome, before the church was transformed; Borromini's initial project; and its final form (1653–57).
187. Plan of the Finnish Pavilion at the New York World's Fair of 1939, by Alvar Aalto: a diagonal, undulating composition.
Following pages:
188–92. Interior view and cross section of Sant'Agnese in the Piazza Navona, and plan of the Palazzo della Sapienza, with the church of Sant'Ivo, by Borromini. *Below:* the Finnish Pavilion in New York (1939) and elements in wood, by Alvar Aalto.

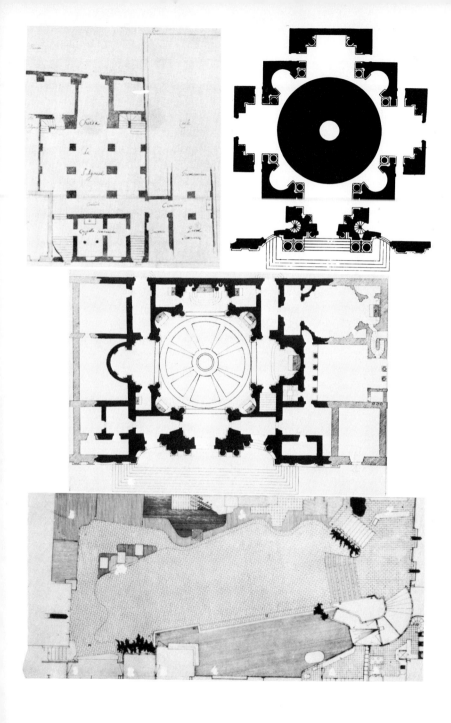

that is, to the additive process: church + pendentives + cupola + lantern. Where is the cupola in Sant'Ivo? It no longer exists. Its springline is one with the cornice of the chamber below; therefore the cupola heightens the building, yet sinks its roots into it. It represents a total reintegration, as in the Pantheon, but an anticlassic reintegration which sunders regular space. Indeed, Sant'Ivo's geometric matrix is unrecognizable. The hexagon of the floor has no spatial effect because its sides are molded in concave and convex shapes. Centrifugal forces not only alternate with centripetal impulses, but they are hindered in their thrust toward the outside. The triangles, in the form of the Star of David, do not altogether fit into the plan, yet they indicate a hypothetical geometry which, passing through the envelope of the church, finds its completion only outside the envelope. Borromini's genius made this miracle possible by imbuing a central organism with thrilling dynamism.

Every aspect of the Baroque language answers the same purpose. Consider, for example, the question of vertical communication. During the Renaissance, the stairway, a separate product of decomposition, was encaged in a recess because its continuity in height was considered incompatible with the superimposition of the orders. Even in the full tide of the sixteenth century, the stairway in the Palazzo della Sapienza was relegated to one of the many rectangles that divide the structure; it is therefore wholly hidden from the courtyard, and it leaves no mark on the façade. This system came to an end with the helicoid of the Palazzo Farnese in Caprarola, anticipated by the spiral stairway of the Vatican Belvedere, just as Sant'Andrea prophesied the Gesù. With the advent of the Baroque, the sixteenth-century box opened up. In the loggia of Palazzo Barberini, external space swept into the main entrance, with its vast pincers ramps. It was the first

---

193–95. *Above, left:* elements in undulating wood, by Alvar Aalto. *Above, right:* cross section of Sant'Ivo alla Sapienza, Rome (1642–60), where Borromini reintegrated the church and its cupola, defying Renaissance decomposing methodology *Below:* view of the cupola of Sant'Ivo. The base of the cupola coincides with the trabeation of the church, contrary to Renaissance and Mannerist practice—as, for example, in Santa Maria della Carceri, Prato (cf. 143); the Gesù, Rome (cf. 176); and Borromini's Sant'Agnese in the Piazza Navona, Rome (cf. 188 and 189).

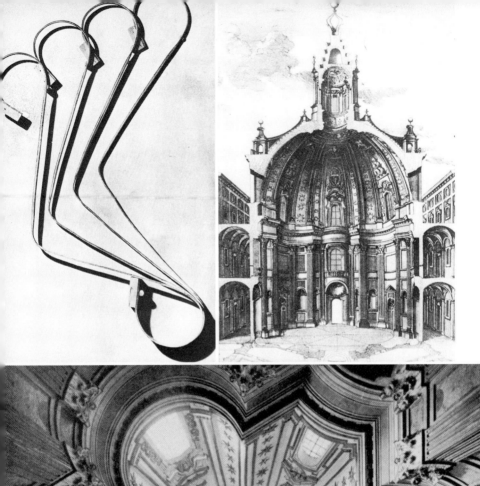

of the grandiose stairways which—from the Palazzo Madama in Turin to Vanvitelli's Reggia in Caserta—demonstrated the vertical reintegration against the broken-up system of the classical orders.

Having seen the architectural components reunified, we pass on to the reintegration of the city and its buildings. Bath, England, projected Borromini's undulating wall on the urban scale. The Baroque serpentine fused cavities, bends, and retreats in endless blocks, unifying the different parts through the agency of light. If one curving section gets the light, the second remains in shadow, the third dazzles, and the fourth stands in the half-light. There are no longer sharp caesuras between dark and light but rather a gradual, homogeneous transition.

The serpentine idea returned to the architectural scene as a feature of the dormitories designed by Aalto for the Massachusetts Institute of Technology. Instead of being confined within an internal vertical tube, the stairs cut across the entire outside wall facing the campus and reunify the superposed floors as they rise. Thus, Aalto created a stairway-corridor that supplanted the habitual decomposing movement in horizontal (corridors) and vertical (stairway) traffic.

The Piazza di Spagna in Rome dispenses with every connotation of the Renaissance idiom. It repudiates the symmetrical void that stamps the Piazza dell'Annunziata in Florence and even the Campidoglio in Rome, bordered by identical buildings, with a church or monument in front and vistas encompassing the whole scene. Separated into two interpenetrating triangles, the Piazza di Spagna blends rhythmically from one into the other. The narrow part in the middle opens up into the Spanish steps, which ascend to Trinità dei Monti, or canalizes into the opposite shaded split of

---

196–99. Altitudinal reintegration in Baroque and organic architecture. *Above:* small stairway in the fifteenth-century Horne House, Florence, attributed to Simone del Pollaiolo, and spiral stairway in the Palazzo Farnese at Caprarola, by Jacopo Barozzi da Vignola (1547–59). *Center:* grand stairway in the Reggia at Caserta, by Luigi Vanvitelli (1752–74). *Below:* stairway-corridors in Aalto's dormitories at the Massachusetts Institute of Technology, Cambridge (1947–48).
Following pages:
200–2. Serpentine volumes. Aalto's MIT dormitories, Cambridge, Massachusetts (1947–48); Landsdown Crescent, Bath (1794); Paper Mill at Fors, by Ralph Erskine (1953).

Via Condotti. An extraordinary, antiperspective invention, this piazza is not a formally isolated component of the city, but rather a magnet for converging and dispersing traffic in various directions.

The Piazza del Quirinale effaces every geometric pattern and rigid stereometry of empty urban space. There is no correlation between its flanks, therefore no symmetry. A void without any strict design, it is the terminus of the long, straight Via XX Settembre (once Strada Pia, outlined by Michelangelo), and the starting point of the descent to the Piazza Venezia and the Corso. Following the direction of the palace's façade, in the distance we can see St. Peter's loom up over the panorama. The surrounding buildings abide by no right-angle rules; therefore their façades give off infinite tonalities and nuances of light. At any hour of the day, the Piazza del Quirinale assimilates and conveys the total range of light.

Nothing can be reintegrated before it has been decomposed. The Baroque urban continuum detached façades from the buildings in such a way that they became mere street backdrops. Two examples of this, among many, are the fronts of Sant'Agnese, Piazza Navona, where Borromini curved the wall expanse, and the basilica of Santa Maria Maggiore, with its broad, palpitating arches emphasized by the side strips. The San Carlino façade negates the corner of the Quattro Fontane in order to emphasize the street axis. The convexities of Sant'Ivo's drum are in dissonance with the concave lower part of the church, which is connected with the sixteenth-century portico. To achieve reintegration, the compact Renaissance volume was attacked by the double assault of internal spaces and urban continuum.

Organic architecture relates to the rationalism of the 1920s and 1930s just as did the Baroque to the Renaissance. It was the same

203–8. *Above:* aerial view and plan of the Piazza di Spagna, Rome, formed by two triangles joining at their apexes. *Center:* aerial view and a 1676 drawing of the Piazza del Quirinale, Rome, conforming to the directions of the urban traffic flow, hence free of geometric preconceptions and parallel alignments. *Below:* two details of Boston's City Hall Plaza, by Paul Rudolph, a project influenced in part by medieval urban centers and, to a great extent, by the dynamic schemes and kinetic values of the Baroque cities (1963–71).

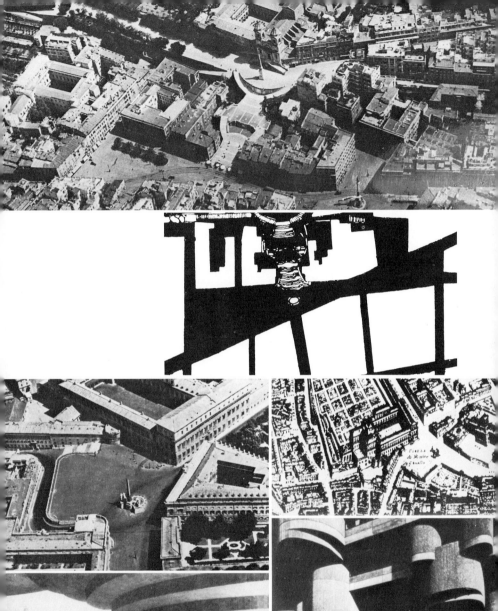

linguistic phenomenon, but with a notable difference: the Baroque reintegrated the three Renaissance dimensions, while the organic reintegrates the four dimensions of Cubism. The Baroque was concerned with undulating walls and street backdrops; organic architecture with spaces and volumes of the city-region.

From the beginning of our century, Frank Lloyd Wright—profiting from a rationalist experience that matured in the United States thirty years ahead of Europe—became the prophet and genius of the organic trend. He extolled the horizontal, the ground line, unfinished materials sometimes crude and telluric, and the house anchored in the soil as a factor of a reintegrated landscape. From the language of his master, Louis H. Sullivan, he removed every classical residue, such as isolated volumes, waxed surfaces, sharp contours, crystal purity, and abstract geometrics. In the Roberts House (1908) in River Forest, Illinois, Wright built a living room two stories high. Forty years later, for the Guggenheim Museum in New York, he designed a grand helicoidal ramp to serve as both a stairway-corridor and a street-structure.

Compared with present-day architecture, including the most daring works, the high spots of organic poetics—Wright's Falling Water (1936) in Bear Run, Pennsylvania; the Johnson Building in Racine, Wisconsin; and Taliesin West, Arizona—belong to the future. They incorporate all the invariables of the modern code: listing, dissonances, antiperspective three-dimensionality that discounts Cubist doctrines; four-dimensional decomposition, with Wright as the father of De Stijl neoplasticism; cantilevered structures, with Falling Water as their supreme example; space-in-time; and reintegration of building, city, and landscape. Fifty years before anyone else, Wright foresaw that the automobile would destroy the traditional antinomy between urban nuclei and the

---

209–12. Reintegration of land- and cityscape in the Baroque period and in the organic architectural trend. Aerial view of Santa Maria Maggiore, Rome, with the façade by Ferdinando Fuga, inserted into the building block (1736). Three works by Frank Lloyd Wright: Midway Gardens, Chicago (1914); Taliesin West, Arizona (1938); Price House, Bartlesville, Oklahoma (1955).
Following pages:
213–15. Piazza Navona in Rome, with the curvature of Sant'Agnese in Agone, by Borromini. Two views of the Johnson Administration Building, Racine, Wisconsin, by Wright (1936).

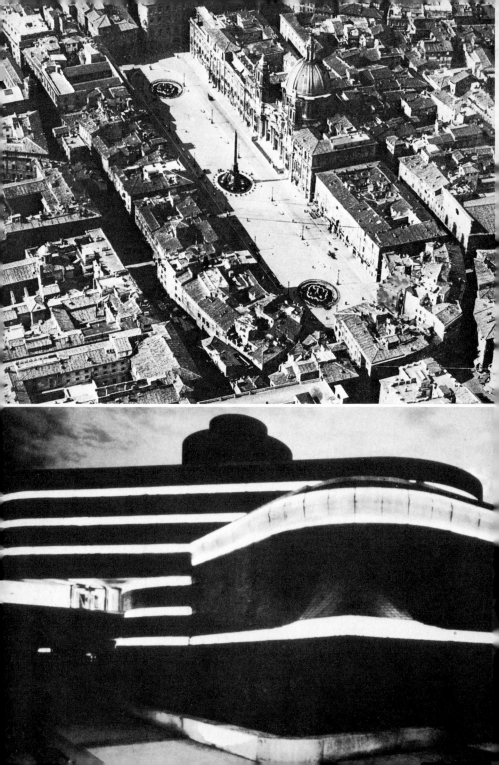

countryside. In his Broadacre City project, he proposed urbanizing the entire region, providing for fulcrums of powerful density vertebrated by mile-high skyscrapers that hark to the future.

The principle of reintegration qualifies every valid contribution today. Two examples are Habitat '67 in Montreal, by Moshe Safdie, and John Johansen's Mummers Theater in Oklahoma City. Both structures, assemblages of cells and communication tubes, are open, unfinished, absorbing the city space within their organisms in an uninterrupted dialogue of internal, external, private, and public voids. With Wright, a new architectural language was born. However exasperatingly slow its assimilation may be, it has put its stamp on all contemporary research and trends.

216–17. Spatial temporizing and reintegration in Sant'Ivo alla Sapienza, Rome (1642–60), by Francesco Borromini. Spatial temporizing and building-city reintegration in the Guggenheim Museum, New York (1946–59), by Frank Lloyd Wright. For a comparison between the helicoids of these two works see 30 and 31. The extraordinary affinity between Borromini and Wright is particularly surprising in that the genius of Taliesin almost ignored the Baroque master.

Preceding pages:
218. Aerial view of Matera, in southern Italy, with the inhabited areas known as "I Sassi"—a dramatic document of prehistoric life that has survived to the present.
Above:
219. A night view of Las Vegas, striking example of a culture reduced to the nadir: Pop architecture and Pop planning.
Following pages:
220–21. A primitive village of the Dogon tribe in Mali, West Africa. *Barriadas* in Lima, Peru, today.

Conclusion:
Prehistory and the Zero Degree of Architectural Culture

Historiography, revivals, and the modern language are the three keys we have used to examine the architectural evolution from the monuments of ancient Greece to the Baroque period. We have seen that, on the one hand, erudite probes into the past have incited orgies of stylistic eclecticism, whose only merit has been to overthrow the despotism of neoclassicism. On the other, however, research into history has nurtured modern culture with a feedback, the more incisive the less it is evident.

What now remains is to review the eons of prehistory, the architecture of hundreds of thousands of years before the invention of writing. Side by side with recorded history, prehistory has continued to exist. It is with us even today in countries still technologically primitive, in backward rural areas, and, to some extent, in the anonymous buildings of the city slums—in short, wherever professional architects are, and have been, missing, and kitsch dominates the scene. Here is an immense patrimony that ranges over millennia, from the primitive settlements of paleolithic times to the gaudy neon signs of Las Vegas, encompassing vernaculars, spontaneous, exotic idioms and dialects, language forms extraneous to the official codes. Even shanty towns implanted on mounds of refuse deposited by our industrial society can be considered primitive entities, brought to our aesthetic attention by Pop Art.

Interest in prehistory and primitive architecture has mounted considerably over the past decades. Why? Once again, the motives are both creative and critical. The study of regions, landscapes, and minor settlements and the growth of urban research have

led us to recognize the values of "architecture without architects," of humble environments and simple social fabrics. Unless we know and understand them, we shall fail to grasp the context that underlies the emergence of major monuments. Indeed, there are sublime achievements, like the Piazza del Campo in Siena and the Piazza di Spagna in Rome, which boast no buildings of any special importance, and splendid cities, Ferrara for one, created by architects of modest stature. Since modern planning embraces the whole physical gamut of human communities, it is only logical that in its investigations it should include "out-of-time" aggregates, *barriadas* and *favelas,* hovels and shanties—everything that art historians have thus far disdainfully banned from their books.

Architects have another, more profound, reason for consulting prehistory. In an epoch of hasty, feverish building activity, when linguistic codes age without maturing and submit to wanton abuse even before they have been formalized, they revert to the original sources, to the habitat of uncivilized man and the underprivileged who live like aborigines within the metropolitan magma. Sickened by the crude expedients and superficial forms he sees around him, the architect, to use Roland Barthes' terms, descends to the "zero degree" of his culture and tries to adapt his work to the popular idioms. Such a "hippy" operation is pregnant with ambiguities and illusions, yet it is healthy all the same. To be sure, every architectural revolution begins by rejecting the official code and leveling it to the nadir. In different ways and to different degrees, Brunelleschi, Michelangelo, and Borromini did just that. Also Gaudí, inspired by the grottoes of Almeria and the caves; Wright, in the Ocotillo Desert Camp (1927) near Chandler, Arizona; Mendelsohn, when he discovered the "architecture of

222–25. *Above:* Neolithic village of Ba Ila in Northern Rhodesia. *Center:* two views of geodesic domes in the "hippy" community of Drop City in Trinidad, Colorado. *Below:* Habitat '67, Montreal, by Moshe Safdie.
Following pages:
226. Matmata village in southern Tunisia, with craters converted into living quarters: underground cavities put to domestic use by cavemen.
227–31. "Architecture of the dunes," five sketches by Erich Mendelsohn, dated 1920. The Expressionist vision finds incentives in a landscape constantly varied by the sweeping wind.

dunes"; and Le Corbusier who, at Ronchamp, denied the five principles laid down in 1921. Safdie, too, demolished the prevailing code when he transplanted a Middle Eastern village into Canada together with the community spirit of the Kibbutz, and Johansen when he piled junk upon junk to build his Mummers Theater. In the same category we can also include the works of the *informel* trend, the pseudotroglodytic volumes and "sculptured spaces" of André Bloc, the open-ended structures by Frederick Kiesler, Claude Parent's oblique projects, and the so-called "earth architecture."

More and more we train our sights on prehistory as our illusions about the future of the technological society ebb away, as we awake to the extent of the ecological disasters besetting our planet, to the gigantism that alienates man from his fellow men and his surroundings, to the bureaucratic process by which the individual is reduced to a conformity deprived of quality. Modern painting nods approval of primitive gestures and instant actions. Alberto Burri and Robert Rauschenberg exhibit rags in sophisticated museums. Modern music welcomes the aesthetics of noise and aleatory techniques. The young exist by improvisation and clothe themselves in tatters in the belief that they are bringing art into their lives.

Psychoanalysis and anthropology examine the behavior, totems, symbols, and taboos of primitive peoples to single out those elementary and instinctive needs that mechanized civilization has repressed. In architecture, too, the "zero degree" means to repose all the basic questions, much as if we were to build the first house in history. Is the metropolitan aggregate, jam-packed with millions of dwellers, compatible with the survival of the individ-

---

232–33. Two views of the Mummers Theatre, Oklahoma City (1971), by John Johansen: architectural conventions demolished, an assemblage of scraps and wreckage, "action architecture" built out of "pieces and circuits."
Following pages:
234. Dwellings at Metameur, southern Tunisia, which repropose man's prehistoric existence in natural caves.
235–36. Villa "a rajada" near Gland, Switzerland, by Robert Frei, Christian Hunziker, and Henry Presset (1961). Model for a recreational center near Chambéry, Savoie, by Pascal Häusermann (1967).

ual? What are the limits of social tolerance beyond which economic development becomes suicidal? Do the paths and tracks of the archaic village postulate the geometric street chessboard, subsequently canonized by Hippodamus of Miletus, or are we better off with systems that discard right angles and squares? Does Wright's principle, "the house as shelter," reflect the urgency of our forebears to go underground, a desire evidenced repeatedly over the centuries in subterranean temples, in the catacombs, in Renaissance and Baroque grottoes, and in contemporary basement nightclubs? Or is the principle of pilotis, the house on stilts, championed by Le Corbusier, more valid, as prehistoric pile dwellings seem to show? And again: does not the wall enveloping interior space without panels juxtaposed at right angles and stitched together—as we find in Capri, Positano, Ravello, and Amalfi; in the domed roofs of the Ligurian Riviera; and in the cone-shaped stone *trulli* of Apulia—offer an organic unity preferable to Renaissance and De Stijl decomposition? And does not the fusion of house and street, as in the cave dwellings of Matera, suggest a precedent for the trend toward reintegration? Do not the dolmens and menhirs strewn over prehistoric sectors, and the mysterious ruins of Stonehenge in England, testify that monumentality is deeply rooted in the human soul?

Architects are assailed by innumerable questions that demand scientific answers. This is not a matter of regressing to romantic attitudes out of a mystical fascination with a legendary past but, on the contrary, of putting the dialogue between art and criticism on a systematic basis. This dialogue requires energy and courage, a rereading of prehistory and history so that we can write and speak the modern language of architecture.

---

237. Model for the Roosevelt Memorial, Washington, D.C., by William F. Pederson and Bradford S. Tilney. This project won the 1960 competition: a crown of "prehistoric" stelae with platforms creating an altitudinally staggered podium.
Following pages:
238. Aerial view of the so-called Temple of the Sun at Stonehenge, near Salisbury. This most spectacular of all prehistoric monuments is ascribed to the era between 1800 and 1400 B.C. When interest in prehistory is immune from nihilist romanticism, it offers a valid and fertile source of verification for modern architecture.

Index

Photographic Sources